THE SUCCESS COACH

How to Design, Launch + Grow Your Coaching Business

Samira Toussi

ISBN 13: 979-8-9854063-3-7 (hard cover)
ISBN 13: 979-8-9854063-4-4 (soft cover)

To my dad,
who always pushed me to do my own thing.
Always believed in me.
Empowered me to make my own choices.
And only saw my strengths.

And to my mom,
who exemplifies curiosity, creativity and charisma.
I am me, because of you.

TABLE OF CONTENTS

PHASE IV:
COACHING NECESSITIES 2 I IN SESSIONS

INTRODUCTION

You were born to be a coach and help as many people as you can, guide others, elevate their game and inspire them to reach their highest potential.

So ultimately, you know you want to help others live extraordinary lives...

But let me ask you this:

- Are you stuck on how to start and grow a coaching business?
- Do you feel overwhelmed by all the things you need to start a business, like a website, blog, and social media?
- Do you lack clarity in how to design your consulting/coaching business, such as finding a niche and designing your package?
- Are you working hard but still have few to no clients?
- Do you lack confidence in your skills as a coach and feel unsure of how to refine your approach?
- Are you missing the tools to take your business to the next level?

If the answer to any of these questions is a yes, then this is THE book for you.

I've put all my years of experience in coaching and creating learning experiences into this book to make creating a coaching business simple, to make it doable and to make it work. Is that even possible?

Trust me, by the end of this book, you'll be saying F*CK YEAH!

In this book, you will understand the step-by-step blueprint to starting a coaching business with confidence, ease, and simplicity!

With this book, you will:

- Have the systems and processes to attract consistent clients and income.
- Know how to structure your coaching business, including packages, sessions and your ideal coaching niche.
- Feel credible and prepared to build and grow your business.
- Have a proven structure to make your first to last coaching session powerful.
- Feel confident in your ability to get your clients real results.
- Learn how to attract more of the clients (that you want!).
- Learn how to create a social marketing strategy and collaborate with others for business development.
- Structure the operations of your business to win back time and set boundaries with your efforts (remember, you started your business for more flexibility!).
- Master the coaching toolbox of asks to run your client through your entire coaching process.
- Utilize proven life coaching best practices including step-by-step processes and powerful tools.
- Polish your communication techniques so that you can listen and question your clients to success.
- Know how to set expectations, maintain boundaries, and overcome your own fears around coaching.
- Have access to professional done-for-you forms and templates that take the guesswork out of the coaching process.
- Work with your clients to set achievable goals and action plans and hold them accountable to follow through.
- Develop your emotional intelligence and a growth mindset.
- Help your clients eliminate limiting beliefs and stop holding themselves back.

- Help your clients make hard decisions and feel moti-vated to take actions they've been putting off.
- Help your clients live a life of passion and purpose.
- Discover your ideal coaching niche and design your coaching package.
- Learn secrets to attract clients and market your coach-ing business to be the most successful yet.

So remember, whether it is day 1 or day 1000 of your coaching business, we can ALL benefit from a pause to reflect, plan and prioritize the actions to build and grow your coaching business.

So grab a cup of hot tea, dig into the chapters and appendices and let's get started!

See you on the other side!

Love,
Sami

BUT FIRST, WHO AM I?

As a little girl...

...I always knew I was meant to do something to help others. But as I moved into my adulthood, I felt the need to follow the safe path of earning good grades, being a "go-getter" and following all the rules. I made sure I was always a "good girl," seeking validation in a way that earned me praise by pleasing everyone but myself.

At 25 years old...

...I landed a career in a prestigious, male-dominated field in the corporate sector. I moved around the organization in operations, business development, marketing and project management. I was doing it all! And before I knew it, I was an expat living in Dubai, making six-figures, managing and training a large team, leading board meetings and traveling around the world. On the outside, it looked like I had it figured out - but on the inside, I knew I wasn't living my purpose.

Despite feeling unhappy...

...I continued to stay at my unfulfilling job in order to gain outside approval. I constantly measured my worth and success by comparing myself to others and would question everything, "Am I earning enough?" "What do people think of me?" "Will my family agree with this choice?"

I came to the realization...

...that my life didn't really belong to me. I had spent the last decade obsessed with personal growth - reading books, taking psychology courses, listening to podcasts, and studying human behavior, fascinated by what makes people "successful." So why was my own success so unfulfilling?

I finally broke when...

...these internal doubts began to manifest themselves through my physical and mental health. I decided it was enough. It was time to make a change and that meant redefining what "success" meant to ME, not to OTHERS. So, I did exactly that. I pressed pause on my story so I could start a new one.

I changed my definition of "success" and channeled my passion, education and skills into something that brought me, and the people I now serve, purpose.

Focused on Real Results

With over 10,000+ hours as a Business and Life Strategist, I've worked with hundreds of entrepreneurs and coaches to embark on entrepreneurial journeys and grow successful businesses. This book has helped my clients with just a few of the following:

- launching their website
- tripling their income
- hitting $25K a month
- launching products
- partnering with multi-million dollar franchises
- and more.

This book uses science-based techniques and the tools that have helped me to set you up with solid, actionable plans and reach measurable success.

Licensed & Certified

My studies began with a BA in International Development from UCLA. I then earned Board-Certification in Life & Business Coaching from the acclaimed Tony Robbins Strategic Interventionist School and Executive Coach Training Program, CCF in

2015. Today, I have conducted 10,000+ hours of coaching, and run 70+ workshops across the world on my signature RPP (Reflecting, Planning, Prioritizing) Method to help entrepreneurs launch their business. Obtaining the best possible coaching education has helped me create actionable strategies proven to help people gain clarity and confidence to execute.

BASIC FOUNDATION - VALUES & VISION

Phase I discuss the foundation of your business. Before you officially launch your coaching business, there are details of your business that need to be outlined. We start by getting to know the who, what and why of your business. This includes reviewing your ideal client, their challenges, how your business offers them a solution and solidifying your elevator pitch. Next, we review your strengths as a coach, crafting your personal bio and creating a package or program to set you up for long-term success. Once you have these topics solidified, you'll be able to go into the next phase of your business!

1

The Business Bible

The Business Bible, or Business Canvas is the first introductory tool used to define and communicate your business idea. It helps you describe and assess a business model, encompassing components such as: customer segments, value propositions, channels, customer relationships, revenue streams, key resources, key activities, key partnerships and cost structure.

Use the one-page document in Appendix A to work through the fundamental elements of your business to help you structure your ideas in a coherent way which supports your vision of what's to come next.

- **Step 1: Customer Segment** - Focus on just one type of customer segment to start. Think about their age, gender, occupation, personality... Who do you want to work with? Note: Don't be afraid of losing out on clients, you want to be a specialist not a generalist - there are too many coaches out there trying to do it all!
- **Step 2: Early Adopters** - Think, who will be the first type of person to buy your service? If they are professionals: let's focus on the specific industry they are in, ie. tech, healthcare, legal. Thinking about this will be

the easiest path to identifying your customer segment. Note: If you can't get them to buy your product, it'll be harder to get others.

- **Step 3: Problems** - Identify the top three pain points for your customer segment. Why do they need your product/service?
- **Step 4: Existing Alternative** - How is this problem being solved now?
- **Step 5: Solution** - Describe how you would solve these top three problems with specific solutions.
- **Step 6: Unique Value Proposition (USP)** - Represents a promise you make to your customers to get noticed. Craft this around your top problem and finished story benefit.
- **Step 7: High-Level Concept** - Single statement to describe your idea. i.e. Youtube=Flickr for videos.
- **Step 8: Key Metrics** - What's your minimum success criteria? Keep this criteria at 3 years or less.
- **Step 9: Channels** - What are some paths to get your customers to adopt your product/service?
- **Step 10: Revenue Streams** - Start thinking about revenue sources to come up with a rough pricing model.
- **Step 11: Cost Structure** - Estimate your runway to get started. What are some of the initial expenses you will have?

Toussi's Top Takeaways:

- Follow the numerical structure in the business canvas to help you tackle the most important business foundations first and reach clarity in next steps.
- When you get to section Unique Value Proposition (UVP), think about how you would describe this business to your mom or grandmother; remember: the simpler the statement, the better.

- Reflect on the metrics that will help you feel successful in your business. This may include criteria such as net profit, leads per month, customer loyalty, work-life balance.
- Remember, most importantly you are always dating your ideas - you're allowed to change your mind as your business evolves.

See Appendix A - Business Canvas

2

Who Is Your Ideal Client?

Having a niche is key. You may argue that this narrows your market and decreases the number of potential clients, but what it actually does is enable you to appeal to an audience that truly values what you do. The more you come to know your ideal client, the easier it will be for you to create content that speaks directly to them. When a potential client feels like you "get them," your offer becomes so much more appealing. But both identifying and finding your ideal customer is not always easy.

Our goal is to target your ideal customer messaging across every aspect of your business, from your website to your elevator pitch. First, however, we need to answer questions that help you clarify who this customer is, their values, their struggles and how they spend their time. Use the ideal client review to get to know that dream customer.

Know that this process can take time, and it's a tough one. But the process of identifying your ideal customer will help you solve tons of business challenges from marketing to promotion, to effective speaking, to networking. It takes some time in the beginning but once you get it, it's the gift that keeps on giving! The framework in Appendix B allows you to reflect on key components to identify who your ideal client is, as well as providing you with examples to start thinking about how your client behaves, ensuring business success.

Toussi's Top Takeaways:

- The ideal client will be loyal to your company, frequently uses or buys your products or services and is likely to recommend you to their friends and colleagues.
- Think about someone you've helped in the past, what were their interests? Or, if you haven't worked with anyone, who do you enjoy helping?
- I'm often asked, "How do I find my niche?" Many times your niche is people similar to you! Reflect on your passions and interests or think about your best friend. What are their passions?
- Think about which areas you have special skills or experience in What do people regularly tell you you're good at? What's your training or education in? What special skills or knowledge have you developed through your work? Use these to craft the niche for your early adopters.

See Appendix B - Ideal Client Review

3

Uncovering Your Elevator Pitch

Before you can begin to sell your product or service to anyone else, you have to sell yourself on it. This is especially important when your service is similar to other services around you. Look around you: How many consultants, coaches, therapists, healers, physicians and other service based companies are out there? How many are truly unique? Very few businesses are one-of-a-kind, and that's ok, but how are you going to make yours stand out?

The key to effective selling in this situation is what advertising and marketing professionals call a "unique selling proposition" (USP). Unless you can pinpoint what makes your business unique in a world of homogeneous competitors, you cannot target your sales efforts successfully.

Pinpointing your USP requires some hard soul-searching and creativity. One way to start is to analyze how other companies use their USPs to their advantage. This requires careful analysis of other companies' ads and marketing messages. If you analyze what they say they sell, not just their product or service characteristics, you can learn a great deal about how companies distinguish themselves from competitors.

The USP is also often the first bit of copy you'll see above the fold on a given company's homepage. It's typically a single sentence-length headline, and is sometimes accompanied by a sub-headline. The essential word in the phrase is "unique." The USP defines your position in the market insofar as it answers the question: What's the ultimate point of differentiation between you and your competitors that makes your company the one worth doing business with?

Before you start thinking about which qualities set your business apart from similar companies, you need to know almost everything about your perfect customer (which you may not know just yet!).

When you're identifying your ideal prospect, consider the following:

- What does your perfect customer really want?
- How can your product or service solve their problem(s)?
- What factors motivate their buying decisions?
- Why do your existing customers choose your business over your competitors?

Remember – it's not enough to merely target a rough demographic. You need to know exactly who you want to sell to and why. Once you know this, you can get to work on the next unique selling proposition best practice, which is...

Consumers don't want to buy products – they want to solve their problems. This could be as simple as purchasing a reliable set of tools that will last for years, but it can (and frequently is) much more complex.

Take the cosmetics industry, for example. Companies in this space don't just sell make-up – they sell lifestyle ideals; glamor, confidence, and style. Think about this in a problem-solving context; people who may not feel glamorous, confident or stylish will if they use a particular product. This lies at the heart of most cosmetics advertising, and this concept applies to many other industries, too.

To create a strong USP, you have to examine the profile of your perfect customer and then market your products in a way that shows them you can meet their needs and solve their problems. You can't hope to write persuasive, compelling copy in the voice of the customer unless you know who they are. If your prospective customers choose your products, how will their lives be improved? What makes your business so different that prospective customers should choose your products or services? The answers to these questions should form the bedrock of your USP. See appendix C to brainstorm your unique selling proposition and feel confident the next time you describe what you do!

USP Examples:

1. Domino's: You get fresh, hot pizza delivered to your door in 30 minutes or less or it's free.
2. Robinhood: An investing platform that believes the financial system should work for everyone, not just the wealthy.
3. Toussi International: Build a successful coaching practice in less than one month.

Toussi's Top Takeaways:

- What you sell doesn't need to be unique (you don't need to reinvent the wheel), but the message that you choose to focus on needs to be unique!

- **USP Formula:** End Result Customer Wants + Specific Period of Time + Address the Objections.
- Your USP plays to your strengths, is targeted and should be memorable.
- Be tangible. Your message has to be backed by everything that you do.
- Be customer-focused. It must showcase a feature or benefit that customers value and want.
- Avoid using empty buzz words to describe your business - you are not yet an established business like Apple or Nike. First your audience needs to understand what you do.
- Your USP should be short, like a Twitter feed, don't let it exceed 140 characters.
- Beta-test your USP, speak it out loud to friends and family. Remember you are not married to your initial decision - you are just dating your ideas. Your USP can change over time.

See Appendix C - Unique Selling Proposition

4

The Top 40 Q's to Business Launch

The Business Questionnaire in Appendix D is a tool to research, brainstorm and ideate further about your business model. At this point, you've completed your business canvas and are ready to move into more detail about the who, what and why of your business. Don't worry, though, there are no "right answers." So even if you haven't done everything you want to or haven't even started, view this as an opportunity to begin brainstorming.

The questionnaire in Appendix D is meant to support you in answering what you can to use as a jumping off point for further ideation and execution. You can use this to set up attainable marketing/business development goals and action items for you going forward. The more information you share, the more thorough you can be in months to come with business growth.

Toussi's Top Takeaways:

- Don't feel intimidated by these questions, let this be the time you research and think about the goals of your business.
- These questions should help you gain insights that allow you to make well-informed business decisions and maximize the potential of your business.
- Use these questions to help you consider your marketing and business development strategy.
- It's okay if you leave half this questionnaire blank. Come back to it when you've dived deeper into your business and had some time to reflect on marketing interests.

Key Questions:

1. What do you think other businesses are missing? What is the industry failing to offer its clients right now?
2. Who do you consider to be your main competitors?
3. What types of content are you most interested in developing? Written? Video? Social media?
4. When it comes to marketing tasks, which do you find least painful to do?(!) – or: what are you most interested in trying?
5. What types of clients do you most enjoy working with? What types of clients do you "click" with the most? Why do you think that is?

See Appendix D - Business Questionnaire

5

Finding that 'Special Sauce'

First, a definition: Your "unfair advantage" is the skill you have that is your unique talent. It might even be why someone chose to invest in you or in your idea. For clients, your unfair advantage could represent why you are the best person for the job at hand. Your unfair advantage is also your unique ability: Do you ever receive a compliment that you just shrug off because whatever is mentioned is just "easy" for you or something you regard as mere common sense? Do you find that there is a particular theme or topic that people consistently come to you with, or seek your consultation about? Is there a type of project or task that ignites your passion, motivates you and is something you can go on and on about? That's your unfair advantage.

That's your natural talent, your unique ability - the things you do where you're passionate, energetic, feel like there's never-ending room for improvement and what people know you for! Your unfair competitive advantage could be your community, network, past experience (i.e. if you want to become a business coach and used to be a recruiter or in HR). It is something that cannot be easily copied or bought by your competitors.

This unfair advantage will help you build trust and credibility with clients and prospective clients. Unfair advantage examples could include your past experience, books you've published, insider information and more. Honing-in on what this is will also increase your own confidence and help your pitch when meeting prospective clients.

The personal bio is your story of how you started your business, the journey you were on prior to your business and the mission behind creating your business. Remember, learning how to write a bio is not easy; defining yourself in a few words even less so. But never fear—you **can** do it! Remember, you'll want to include your name, company, goals and aspirations, 2-3 most impressive and relevant achievements and quirky facts about you (if it's appropriate to the site).

Toussi's Top Takeaways:

- Reflect on why your client would trust you. What do you have to offer that other businesses don't?
- Your unfair competitive advantage could be your community. Think of who your network is and how you can utilize them to assist your clients.
- Unfair advantage examples could include your past experience (i.e. if you want to become a business coach and used to be a recruiter or in HR), books you've published (or intend on publishing), insider information and more. It is something that cannot be easily copied or bought by your competitors.
- When drafting your business bio, think about your personal story and what your ideal client needs to know about your story.

- In the business bio, remember to introduce yourself, include professional achievements and discuss your passions and company values. Don't be afraid to personalize it with a few personal details. Have a hobby you love? A favorite book? A professional hero you look up to? Add them to give your potential clients a taste of who you are before they work with you.

See Appendix E - Unfair Competitive Advantage

6

Becoming The Unstoppable Coach: How to Create a Coaching Program

Single sessions? Bundle package? Or a full fledged program?! If you're looking for long-term results, success stories or financial security, a coaching program is key. Take it from me, I started working with clients on single-sessions and what I found is that people want quick results. A program helps them see that there are different phases in the process of growth, ultimately helping you help them as best as you can.

A coaching program also creates long-lasting results for your ideal client and for you! It moves you from being a "freelancer" to an "entrepreneur." Why? Programs help you attract more success stories, because you are working with a client for a longer period of time to reach a specific goal, such as building their email list, creating a coaching program, or becoming more attractive to their ideal partner.

A program helps clients to have a clearer idea of what they can expect to accomplish through your work together. It can also increase their confidence in your ability to help them get the results you promise, which keeps them coming back for more or referring you to their network. Use the program framework in Appendix F to help provoke thoughts and ideas about the phase, reflection point, material, and added value of how your ideal customer would get the most success and value out of your sessions together.

Toussi's Top Takeaways:

- A coaching program will move you from "freelancer" to "entrepreneur."
- A program helps clients to have a clearer idea of what they can expect to accomplish through your work together.
- It provides more success stories, resulting in more referrals and continued business growth.
- Ensure every step of the program is intentional and part of the overall result.
- Take-Home materials to support your clients growth are a must - for example, if you're helping a client land a new job, create a worksheet for resume tips & takeaways.

See Appendix F - Program Template

7

Websites Made Simple

A Website Outline is used to prepare the key points and content for every page of your website. Using an outline will ease the process of building your website, ensuring you don't miss any pertinent information. At minimum, the homepage should include the following: 1. Intro (your unique value proposition, above the fold) 2. Services, 3. About Me 4. Contact button.

Additional website pages may include your testimonials, blogs, a longer "about me" section and other resources you want your prospective clients to see.

See Appendix G - Website Outline to organize your content with your ideal customer, USP and unfair advantage notes we've reviewed in earlier sections. Make sure to keep all key material well-organized before designing your site.

Note: Instructions on how to craft your website content and examples of ideas are listed in Appendix G to support your success.

Toussi's Top Takeaways:

- Keep the design simple, fresh and unique. As the first thing potential customers see when they visit your website, the homepage is typically the most important part of a small business's Web design.
- Make sure your homepage answers the critical questions new visitors will be asking, including who you are, what your business is and what they can do on your website.
- Content must be impactful and engaging with many call to action buttons.
- A sitemap will help keep material organized for your designer to place onto your actual website.

See Appendix G - Website Outline Strategy Guide

BUSINESS OPERATIONS
I ON THE BUSINESS

Phase II Business Operations covers the key ingredients to keep your business' "lights on."

This section offers practical and actionable content and resources to support you in business development as well as the simplest steps to optimize your website ranking, attract your ideal clients (not just anyone!) and a structure to your operating system – everything from client onboarding to ensuring you get a kick-ass testimonial and referrals!

Next, we navigate ways to leave your client awe struck by your coaching session, how to set clear client expectations to ensure a successful journey from day one, the top marketing strategies to exponentially grow your business and building a community of entrepreneurs for long-term success.

Lastly, we will close the section with a sales script to ensure you feel confident to on-board the highest number of prospective clients.

The tools and templates in the appendix of the book are the foundation to setting up your business for success and I wish I had these when I started! It would have saved me time and money while helping me build more confidence to go out and do what I love - coach! First, let's take a look at SEO so you can successfully find your ideal client.

8

What's SEO?

After you've established the foundation of your business and set up your online presence, it's time to focus your energy on finding clients. Search Engine Optimization (SEO) is one strong way to increase virtual foot traffic as it uses keywords to bring an audience to your page.

SEO is the process of optimizing your website to get free traffic from search engines like Google. Make sure to set up your website with keywords to attract your ideal client. For example if you're a career coach, write articles on promotions, finding your dream job, resume writing, personal branding and salary negotiation. If you're a mindset coach, make sure you address your client's top challenges, this could be overthinking, lack of presence or negative thoughts.

The SEO Success tool in Appendix H helps you understand what people are searching for online, the answers they are seeking, the words they're using and the type of content they wish to consume. Knowing the answers to these questions will allow you to connect to the people who are searching online for the solutions you offer.

Toussi's Top Takeaways:

- SEO is crucial because it makes your website more visible, and that means more traffic and more opportunities to convert prospects into customers.
- Your website content needs to be clear so that the search engine knows what your company is about.
- Find relevant keywords that people are searching for by putting yourself in the shoes of a potential customer and make sure to include the keywords on your site and in your messaging.
- Block out time to update your site at least twice per month - this includes blogs, new services, events, client testimonials, etc. Remember, any new content will support your SEO ranking.
- Make sure you have both outbound and internal hyperlinks. This can look like linking relevant content material to support your blog, or linking a previously self-published blog to your new blog post.
- When you upload photos to your website make sure to tag them based on what your customers would be searching. For example, if you're a career coach, tag the image as "career coaching," "change jobs," "career transition," "promotion," "higher salary."
- Create a profile on the top online directories such as Google Business, Yelp, Thumbtack, Noomii (a coaching-specific directory that's been around since 2010) and Bark. While you may not use these for lead generation, these highly ranked SEO platforms will help improve your online ranking.

See Appendix H - Mastering SEO

9

Business Launch Party

Toss the confetti—it's your business' birthday! You've been preparing for this day for months, there's been blood, sweat and tears – doubts, nerves and stress that's all played into it. But now it's time to share your results with your people!

Let's celebrate this business launch with an announcement! This should include a direct subject line such as "Launching my business!" or "Business Launch Party!" The email should include how you got into coaching, why you started your own business and call to actions to get your nearest and dearest spreading the word.

Share your enthusiasm with your network, so that they are excited to support you! Don't forget to include social buttons so that your network knows to follow you and can share with their community.

Remember, large brands use email marketing to build hype for a new launch, features or an event. You'll be using this email template to tell your network about the start of your new business. Why is this crucial? Because our family and friends will be our ambassadors to grow the brand. Check out Appendix I for a launch script to share with your community!

Top 5 Checklist:

1. Make a list of contacts: refer to your personal contacts on your phone and email list, as well as those on your social media accounts. Consider who your target audience is and focus on sending the announcements to that market.

2. Decide on a digital announcement: this is the easiest way to communicate to your large audience at once. You could either send a personalized email or BCC all contacts at once.

3. Write an introduction: Effective new business announcements are often brief and clear to a reader, so it's important to limit your introduction to a few sentences. Make sure to include: a personalized greeting that includes the recipient's name, the name of your business and the services your business offers. See Appendix I for an example script.

4. Add a call to action (CTA): Effective business announcements also typically include explicit directions that ask a recipient to complete a desired action. It may be helpful to entice potential customers with an incentive for passing on your email or signing up for a session. For example, a reward can be something such as: The first 10 clients receive two free sessions!

5. Provide your contact information: Before concluding the announcement, consider offering your potential customers multiple ways to contact you if they have questions. Here are a few elements you can include in a conclusion: your name, website address, social media accounts and phone number.

Toussi's Top Takeaways:

- Your friends and family will be your biggest supporters, especially when first getting started.
- Don't wait too long to send your launch email. Remember progress over perfection, you're never going to be 100% "ready."
- Ensure you provide your network with CTAs so they know how to best support you.
- Include links to your website and social media channels so people can learn more about you. If your site isn't ready yet, a one-page marketing tool is sufficient as well as your LinkedIn for a short bio.
- Didn't get any replies? Don'y worry! Send another email! Remember – email is one of many tools in your box. Schedule calls or in-person meetings with your five best friends & family to catch up and share more info about your business.
- If you do intend on sending out an email through an email marketing platform such as Mailchimp or Constant Contact remember the following: Make sure to start with a short greeting, use images or videos to catch your audience's attention, include links to more info, such as a blog post or social link and include multiple CTAs so that it's easy for your audience to take the next step in booking a call with you.

See Appendix I - Business Launch Email

10

Customer Experience Workflow

A workflow is a sequence of tasks that need to be done to complete a goal. It's the way that people get work done – they follow a series of repeatable tasks that are set out in a workflow. In the beginning, know that you will be operating many functions and wearing various hats in your business venture, thus, a workflow is there to help give direction and clarity to many tasks within a business.

Let's look at Appendix J - the Customer Experience Workflow. This helps you structure the operations of working with your customers. Set this up early in your business to optimize workflow, reduce errors, improve collaboration, acknowledge the business value and reduce time to market, saving the business time and money. This operational tool will help you to set up strong operational standards for the policies, procedures, and protocols you follow in each phase of working with your clients.

Appendix J digs into the most optimal strategies to ensure a successful client journey, starting with the initial consult call and ending with a customer retention strategy. This section will allow you to follow a timing and action guideline for the pre-onboarding, on-boarding, before sessions, in sessions and post-session steps to ensure success.

Toussi Top Takeaways:

- Your client experience workflow will benefit you in setting clear client boundaries and help you stay organized with your optimal workflow.
- Ensure consistency in how things are done, especially in customer-facing situations to make onboarding of customers easier.
- Identify steps that can be automated or streamlined with the right technology.
- New client? The on-boarding process includes the coaching agreement and invoice. Both agreement and payment must be made before starting. No exceptions.
- Carve out 15 minutes before the session to read through your session notes and spend 10 minutes at the end of the call to make sure your notes are in order. You'll thank yourself for this buffer time before your next client meeting!
- Share the evaluation form + testimonial request two to three sessions before the client's final session for sufficient feedback time.
- Closing out your sessions? If they don't sign up for a continued program, insert a check-in call within 30-90 days to see how they are doing.

See Appendix J - Customer Experience Workflow

11

Powerful Coaching Sessions: Revealed

Now that you finalized your customer experience workflow, it's time to define how you'll run your coaching sessions. Why do you need this? As a new coach, this is a fundamental, proven system that you could use to consistently create structure and results for your clients.

As you start working with your ideal clients, you want to make sure you help them hit their maximum potential, which means they need your full support along the way. I say that from my experience. My personal methodology in Appendix K has helped me create maximum results for my clients and supported my own work-life balance to feel prepared and confident for sessions.

When embarking on your coaching-client sessions as a life, career, relationship, business or spiritual coach, you may be hired for helping your clients with confidence, vision, goals or a specific area of life. Use the guide in Appendix K to act as your checklist on how to successfully conduct powerful coaching sessions for your clients.

You can use the tool in Appendix K to check off your presence and operations before, during and after coaching sessions.

Toussi Top Takeaways:

- The *4 fundamentals* of coaching sessions are:
  - Build rapport
  - Setting goals and intentions
  - Coaching through challenges
  - Committed action and accountability
- **Build rapport**: Acknowledge your clients, start with a light conversation, make them comfortable, keep eye contact consistent, open your body language, smile, be genuine, celebrate small wins and share personal stories
- **Setting goals and intentions**: What would make this session successful for you today?
- **Coach through challenges**: Understand the why behind the goal, nail the problem first, stay present, take pauses, note what they say and how they say it. Reflect on patterns in their story. Challenge any belief or behavior that isn't serving them
- **Committed action and accountability**: Always recap the key points of the discussion, list down clear actionable steps
- To take action help your clients understand:
  - Where to start?
  - What to do next?
  - How to attain the goal?

See Appendix K - Powerful Coaching Checklist

12

The Magic of a Coaching Plan

Starting with a new client can feel nerve-racking. When working with new coaches, I repeatedly get questions such as, "How can I show this client that they made the right choice to work with me? What if I don't provide enough value? What if they don't like our work?"

The Coaching Development Plan (CDP) nips those doubts in the butt. Remember, a coaching-client relationship is double-sided. It is not your job to do all the work. Also, feeling nervous about a new client is completely normal! It's like public speaking– it'll be a little scary at first, but once you start, it'll naturally come together. Remember, your role as a Coach is to listen, guide, strategize and ask powerful questions to help move them forward.

The CDP helps you get a strong understanding of your client's expectations, goals and desires of your relationship. It helps set up your whole coaching program. So when you begin working with a new client, the CDP can be used to set the intention for your work together. When you don't set clear intentions at the start of your journey with a new client, you're opening yourself up to all kinds of trouble. It's a simple step, but when you miss it

- disaster. This has personally cost me hundreds and thousands of dollars because there's no measurable goal to fall back on.

You and your client will be able to see the magic and the results of your work together when the CDP is addressed. Your client will know that you've been supporting them, how you've helped them in the past and how you can help them now and in the future. Setting intentions and reminding your clients of these intentions creates a container for trackable, impactful results. By utilizing the CDP tool in Appendix L, you will have a how-to framework to start your sessions on a strong note, ultimately helping your clients get to the next level in their lives.

Toussi's Top Takeaways:

- Step 1: Start your sessions by reflecting on the results they want to see in your coaching process - For example you can ask "What are the outcomes you expect out of this coaching process?"
- Step 2: Take note of their realistic goals within the duration of the program - make sure
- your client is being SMART - the results are sensible, measurable, attainable, results-oriented and time-bound
- Step 5: Continue your inquiries to set practical and clear intentions. Examples to ask...
  - What is the vision for our work together?
  - How do you prefer to be communicated with? Example: are you okay with me calling you out, do you prefer more questions and then me giving you advice?
  - How will we connect and engage during our time together?
  - Are you 100% committed to this coaching experience?
  - Are you willing to NOT let your fear get in the way?

- Step 4: Revert back to their goals and answers to their inquiries often. Share results once per month and respond to inquiries when they aren't being accountable, making excuses or showing a lack of participation (all of these things can come up!)
- Setting intentions at the start of your client journey and reminding your clients of these intentions creates a container for trackable, impactful results.
- Not using a coaching development plan at the start of your client journey may cost you thousands of dollars in retaining clients.

See Appendix L - Coaching Development Plan

13

Kick Butt with that Social Media Marketing Plan

Now that we've defined how to set up a supporting coaching-client relationship and maximize results for your new client, it's time to focus on finding more clients! With this Social Media Marketing Plan, you'll be able to create a foolproof plan to build brand awareness and target new clients.

A social media marketing strategy is important to summarize everything you plan to do and hope to achieve on your social channels. By using a social media marketing strategy to plan your content in advance, you're able to:

- expand your network and thus find more clients;
- Increase engagement on your social channels;
- sell your services more and
- build brand awareness.

The Social Media Marketing Plan should be used as your guide to create the vision of your marketing channel. It helps you ideate your brand persona;you're able to represent your brand personality and values via social media. By finding your tone of voice and communicating it with your audience on social media, you will influence how people perceive you as a coach.

In other words, it describes **how** we want to communicate to our audience, rather than **what**.

Additional tools in the Social Media Marketing plan include examples of business themes, post ideas, a social media holiday calendar as well as possible social partnerships for reach out. Use the resources in Appendix M to create your own social plan.

Toussi's Top Takeaways:

- The more specific your social media plan is, the more effective it will be. Keep it concise. Don't make it so lofty and broad that it's unattainable or impossible to measure.
- Focus on one channel first and master it, i.e. if you're a career coach, LinkedIn is your optimal channel.
- Use channels such as Later or Buffer to prepare for your social media marketing plan. Later is the all-in-one social marketing platform for the top social networks. It helps you plan, analyze and publish your content in a few clicks — so you can save time and grow your business.
- Discussion points and areas of interest for my business include, "authentically you" "communication" "leadership" as these are parts of being a business owner.. If you're a career coach, these could be "personal branding" "mastering the interview" or "strengths finder"
- Social media should be easy, so make every month a different business theme - add stories and organize it so it relieves stress from you and your audience also knows what to expect.
- It's successful in increasing brand awareness, building engaged communities, selling services, providing social customer service, advertising products and services to target audiences and tracking performance to adjust larger marketing strategies accordingly.

See Appendix M - Social Media Strategy

14

Strategic Partnerships That Boost Your Business

When it comes to running a business, the relationships you make with other companies will help you find even greater success. A strategic partnership is usually a non-competing business that will be able to send you clients. For example, if you're a career coach, a strategic partnership could be a university's career center, online job search platforms such as Indeed and Monster, or even headhunters.

In order to make partnerships work, you have to put yourself out there, let people in to get to know you and be willing to support them too! This could take some courage... but it's worth it. There are many good reasons to enter a strategic partnership: they can increase your revenue, grow your brand awareness, broaden your reach and engage new audiences you didn't have access to before.

The purpose of a partnership email is to strike up a conversation with your desired partner and, ideally, to make an offer they can't refuse. Simple as that. Powerful partnership emails (examples included in Appendix N) are personable, convincing and relevant to the receiver. But above all else, it should make it crystal clear what you're offering, what you hope to receive in return and why this partnership is a good idea for the recipient.

Toussi's Top Takeaways:

- *Be clear about what you need:* once you know what you're looking for, you can search for the partner to suit those goals.
- *Do your research:* Try to make sure the partnership is mutually beneficial by finding a business that needs something you provide. This way, they are more likely to offer you what your company needs in return.
- *Create a contract or agreement:* A typical strategic partnership agreement includes the following: a list of all companies involved, the specific services each provides, the specific terms agreed upon, the duration, the signatures of the responsible parties.

In the email to your desired strategic partner, make sure to include the following:

- An introduction: Who are you? Why should this influencer or company be paying attention to your email?
- A compliment or recognition: Why did you choose them as a potential partner? What do you like about them or their work?
- A request: What do you want them to do for you?
- An offer: What will you do if they fulfill your request?
- A conclusion and call to action: What should they do if they want to discuss the partnership further? Offer two times to connect or even better, a link to your calendar to set up a call.

See Appendix N - Partnership Email Templates

15

5-Steps to Your Best Discovery Call

Now that we've mastered the art of capturing a strategic partnership, what happens when you have a prospective client interested in coaching with you? Drumroll please... enter... the discovery call!

A discovery call is the most crucial part of any sales process. It is a conversation in which you build a relationship with your potential customers and guide them through the transformational journey leading to you making the sale. It's also a good way for both you and the prospect to find out if you are a good match for each other. It provides a platform to show you care about the customer's pain points and the solutions you can provide.

Now, a sales script, listed in Appendix N, helps you remain collected and confident in the discovery call. Every good salesperson has a sales script; yet many believe they won't sound natural if they read from a script. While I agree you should never read directly from a script when selling, (it would sound too robotic) a sales script can greatly improve your results by preparing you with the best questions and lines to say and ask.

Thus, the five scenes in Appendix N run through the intro (greeting) to conclusion (payment) of how to master your discovery call. Over my years of experience growing my six-figure business – these are proven methods to work.

Also, see Appendix M for the ten best practices checklist to ensure a successful discovery call. Both Appendix N and Appendix M will help you close your first client (or second, or third...) with ease and grace and without feeling nervous or sleazy.

Toussi's Top Takeaways:

The sales script helps with these top 6 areas:

- Close your first client (or second, or third...) with ease and grace and without feeling nervous or sleazy.
- Remain confident and collected while selling your coaching packages, just as if it was a "regular" coaching session!
- Get more clients to sign up, so you can spend more time coaching and less time marketing.
- Make sales feel abundant and aligned, without feeling like you have to "give in" and use sleazy marketing tactics.
- Create a Sense of Urgency - The fear of missing out is a very powerful thing. An easy to implement tip to close deals faster is to create a sense of urgency. Put a deadline on the deal and price to give the client an incentive to commit, so they don't miss out. You can do this by creating a temporary price discount or offering a free add-on. Give the prospect the feeling they have the upper hand in the deal.

- Use an empathetic communication style during your discovery call through these three steps:

  1. Mimic – Repeat what the other person said.
  2. Rephrase – Paraphrase their comments to show that you've understood.
  3. Reflect – Put their feelings into words for them.

**See Appendix O - Sales Script
and
Appendix P - Sales Checklist**

COACHING NECESSITIES PART I I ON-BOARDING CLIENTS

Welcome to phase three! You are halfway through starting, growing and feeling confident to build your coaching business. Now that we've run through some steps to attract and win new clients, it's time to uncover the necessary tools to on-board your clients with a functioning easy workflow. The templates in The Appendices of the book will be used to make contact before and after the discovery call and ensure you master the on-boarding process while giving your client the highest quality of service. It's as simple as adding your business logo and branding to allow the tools and templates to guide your success. Using the made-for-you templates will create consistency in your messaging and ease your communication with your clients. The tools in The Appendices are the foundation to setting up your business for success. I wish I had these when I started; it would have saved me time and money while helping me build more confidence to go out and do what I love - coach!

16

Got a Prospective Client Inquiry? Here's What to Do!

Got a new client request? YES! If a prospective client has emailed you wanting to learn more about your coaching business, inquired about pricing or sent over a laundry list of their problems, they need you more than ever **right now**. Make sure to reply within 24 hours of receiving a new inquiry and strike while the iron is hot.

The template titled, "Discovery Call Request" in Appendix Q helps the client feel recognized and appreciated for having reached out and makes it simple to sign up for a 1:1 discovery call, all the while learning more about your business. Remember, use this template to support the automation of your business in order to place energy focusing on your natural talent - coaching, while your business continues to expand and grow.

QC Checklist:

- Reply to a prospective client inquiry within 24 hours.
- Save the email in your "template" folder to save an immense amount of time, money and energy (trust me, you'll thank me for this one!).

- Reuse your subject line to create consistency, track leads and correspondence emails for your records.
- Update your calendar link twice a month or as you see best fit. I recommend using the scheduling platform, Calendly (https://calendly.com/), for prospects to schedule based on your availability.
- Include a link to your website, social media channels and testimonial page so your prospective client can learn more about you before the call.

Toussi's Top Takeaways:

- Step 1: First, call the client if a phone number is shared. If you're afraid of calling, know that they probably won't even answer the phone. Do you answer unknown numbers? Exactly. 85% of the population doesn't either.
- Step 2: Make the body of the message personable and powerful, describe your process so the prospect understands what to expect from the consult. More than likely, it's their first time connecting with a coach. Be concrete and specific.
- Step 3: Make sure you have a link to your calendar to avoid the back and forth scheduling frustrations. This way the prospect has options and calendly is optimized to share the calendar invite to both you and client, with follow up emails and texts to ensure a successful start to your meeting.

See Appendix Q - Discovery Call Request Template

17

The Perfect Response to "I'll think about it...."

If you didn't end your discovery call with a payment confirmation, or felt that the prospective client was hesitant, these script examples will help you seal the deal!

We've all been on a call that's going great, when the prospective client ends by saying, "let me think about it" or "I'm just not sure I have the money."

And if you don't know how to handle that response live, you may have frozen up and hurriedly ended the call, not sure where to go next. These tips will teach you what to do in those situations so that doesn't happen.

Continue to build the relationship just like you would if they had given you a big yes. Keep building the relationship. Like any other sales activity, some companies do follow-up emails better than their peers. See Appendix O for a few post-discovery call follow up email templates to send to your prospective client to get them wanting more!

Toussi's Top Takeaways:

- Include something personable that you connected on - i.e. did they go to the same university? Do they love yoga too?
- List out the benefits they'll get from your program. Revert back to the notes you took during your discovery call - use their own language to list their goals.
- Insert relevant client testimonials - was this prospect a physician? Have you worked with other physicians? Include their testimonial or case study. Don't have a relevant client testimonial? Include a link to all your testimonials!
- Insert the time and place (or link) of the check in call you spoke about -or- if you didn't set up a check in time, give them two times in the next week to check in!
- Did they say no? Put regular ticklers for the client in your contact database and touch base with them. Develop an email relationship and let them know occasionally (not every two days) how you are helping your other happy customers.

See Appendix R - Post-Discovery Call Template

18

Adding Value After the Discovery Call

So you've sent out your post-discovery email, but did you know you can give your prospect the gift of coaching even before they officially sign-up? If a prospective client is hesitant about starting your program, see Appendix S to get them hooked!

Give them a taste of how your coaching methods can provide them value with a teaser tool. First, thank them for opening up about their goals (getting vulnerable isn't easy), then share a teaser worksheet (Appendix S) to grasp a feel for what coaching with you could look like.

Tip? Request that they share this tool back to you before your check-in time to hold them accountable as you would in your coaching sessions. See the teaser tool in Appendix S, Life Purpose Questionnaire, which asks thought-provoking questions to help a client reflect on what's important to them and an example of what the coaching process can look like.

Toussi's Top Takeaways:

- The teaser tool is a benefit to the prospect to understand how you operate your business.
- Reflect on the client's obstacles - are they facing issues with clarity? Relationships? Career? Create a teaser worksheet such as the enclosed that can provide value to their specific pain point.
- Request your client to relay info back to you before your scheduled check-in call. Hold them accountable to start making progress like you would in a coaching session.
- Still didn't sign up? Use this tool to reach out again in 60 days - check in on the goals & values they'd like to honor. Remind them of the importance of filling out the worksheet.

See Appendix S - Add-Value Teaser Worksheet

19

The Ideal Contract

We've reviewed the steps to take after your discovery call and how to add value even before a full coaching session;. now, it's time to focus on what to do when they say yes and the necessary documents that must be reviewed, signed and sealed to create a magical relationship.

First up is the must-send coaching agreement. A coaching contract is mandatory and sets the expectations, rules and tone for the entire coaching journey. The coaching contract is sent to a client once they've agreed to work with you and is typically included in the on-boarding packet. It sets up the start of your journey with clear terms and conditions around contract timeline, session timing, rescheduling, canceling, payment info and both client and coach commitments.

The coaching agreement also includes terms the relationship needs to consider and helps to prevent conflict and disputes in the future and uncertainty when something goes awry. Remember, the client MUST sign the coaching agreement before beginning coaching with you. Appendix T includes an example of a coaching agreement to assist you in creating your own. I recommend hiring a professional attorney to help you draft terms & conditions to feel confident in your contract. While it may be costly, it is a lifetime business investment.

Toussi's Top Takeaways:

- The coaching agreement should have a section for your cancellation policy – as this could be a pain point between a coach/client relationship.
- Ensure you've clarified the timing of the sessions - there are always those clients that go over their allotted time. In order to do this, ensure the coaching agreement states that you will deduct the time they went over from your next session together.
- The duration of the program needs to be clear - if a client goes over their specified time frame, the contract is no longer valid.
- Reward your client for sending you referrals! Offer a complimentary coaching session as an incentive for your client to share your information with others.

See Appendix T - Coaching Agreement

20

The New Client Data Form

What's the second attachment in an on-boarding packet? The client data form. A client information form is used to gather key details about the client before starting the coaching journey. It's typically one to two pages and asks for details such as the following: name, occupation, address, emergency contact, birthday, client goals, current reality, potential obstacles and life vision.

Use the new client data form in Appendix U as a reference point to your on-boarding packet. This is not only to **keep client information details on hand, but also so that interactions with clients can run as smoothly as possible. In the form,** gather information about how they heard about you, income, interests and a fun fact (i.e. favorite movie or book). The information will support your marketing and business efforts and can help capture future clients by understanding more about the clients you are attracting to your business.

Toussi's Top Takeaways:

- The new client data form should be part of the on-boarding package for a new client.

- The data form helps create a single location that keeps client information organized and accessible.
- Ensure you ask their favored form of communication and preferred dates/times to meet.
- Ask them a personal question (favorite TV show, movie, sport) to create rapport early on.
- Request for their birthday and note it down to send a birthday gift to nurture the relationship.
- This data should help you understand the type of client your business is attracting and support future marketing efforts.

See Appendix U - New Client Data Form

21

The Power of a Professional Invoice

A professional invoice template doesn't only act as a reliable record of financial transactions between your company and your clients but it can also help reinforce brand identity and show professionalism in all your business dealings. An invoice is delivered in order to demand payment. It's a legally binding agreement showing both parties' consent to the quoted price and payment conditions.

The invoice acts as a bill of statement between you and your client including the scope of the service, price and payment terms. However, there are other benefits to using invoices such as the following:

- 1. Maintaining records
  The most important benefit of an invoice is the ability to keep a legal record of the sale. This makes it possible to find out when a good was sold, who bought it and who sold it

- 2. Payment tracking
  An invoice is an invaluable tool for accounting. It helps both the seller and the buyer keep track of their payments and amounts owed

- 3. Legal protection
  A proper invoice is legal proof of an agreement between the buyer and seller on a set price. It protects the merchant from fraudulent lawsuits

- 4. Easy tax filing
  Recording and maintaining all sale invoices helps the company report its income and ensure that it's paid the proper amount of taxes

- 5. Business analytics
  Analyzing invoices can help businesses gather information from their customers' buying patterns and identify trends, popular products, peak buying times and more. This helps to develop effective marketing strategies.

Toussi's Top Takeaways:

Make sure the invoice has these main points included:

- 1. A standout header
  - The invoice should be unique - have your own, creative header to make it memorable from others!

- 2. Invoice #
  - Every invoice should have its own unique identifier at the top of the page.

- 3. Company Information
  - Near the top of the invoice, you should include the company's legal name.

- 4. Date
  - One of the most important pieces of information you should include is the actual date of the transaction. This will help to simplify the process of cataloging when products are sold or services are rendered.

- 5. Scope of Work
  - The "meat" of the invoice. It doesn't have to be presented in any particular way but should be fairly easy to read and understand. You'll probably want to include things like: the duration of the project, other inclusions, number of sessions.

- 6. Fees or taxes
  - The biggest takeaway here is to include any extra taxes or fees very near the price of the product or service. That way you can take it all together in the "total amount due" field.

- 7. Total amount due
  - This one's probably the most obvious on the list. You need to include the total amount due in the transaction on your invoice. Not only will this settle the amount, it also serves as a good reference point for you and the customer.

- 8. Transaction terms
  - Inevitably, the transaction will include some important verbiage in the transaction terms. They do not form a compulsory part of a formal invoice, however, to make the terms more apparent, it's a good idea to include them on the invoice so that customers can easily reflect back on them.
  - The terms may include penalties for paying late or not paying in full. There could be additional percentages of the bill due at certain later times. Whatever your company's terms, try to include as much of them as you can on each invoice.

- 9. A unique message on the invoice
  - Set yourself apart with a designated spot for personalized messages. This can be used to say "thank you" to a client or make reference to something unique to the project. Think about when you send a

gift or flowers from an online order, there's usually a place to include a special message to your loved one. Make all your customers feel like loved ones with personalized messages right on the invoice!

- 10. Due date on the invoice
    - The due date should absolutely appear on the invoice and might be the most important item on this list (along with the product description and total amount). This will help keep the process and invoice history organized.

See Appendix V - Invoice Template

22

Payments Made Easy

A credit card (CC) authorization form helps you process transactions without requiring customer permission every time. This form requests that your client keep their card on file. It's especially useful when your client requests a payment plan. Attach the CC authorization form to your invoice to get their information and complete the on-boarding process.

While you don't have to use a CC authorization form, I do highly recommend it to ensure fewer late payments, more predictable cash flow and less pressure on both you and the client. Additionally, life is busy. Between work and running a home, there's a lot for your client to stay on top of. Automated fee payments take one big thing off the to-do list for your busy client, giving them peace of mind that the fee is taken care of without anything for them to do.

Toussi's Top Takeaways:

- The CC authorization form is fantastic for clients who request payment plans. Ensure this is sent with the coaching agreement and invoice with dates of charge.

- The CC authorization form should use language that permits you to charge the customer's card without requiring their permission each time.
- Recurring payments offer many benefits to you including fewer late payments, more predictable cash flow and a set-and-forget strategy for clients.
- It supports enhanced customer loyalty by making payments simple, easy and worry-free.

See Appendix W - Credit Card Authorization Form

COACHING NECESSITIES
PART II I IN SESSIONS

Phase IV Coaching Necessities includes the four ingredients to help your client reflect and set intentions for the coaching engagement. In chapter 23 we'll run through a pre-session form to help your clients better gauge the areas of discussion in your coaching session, helping both you and them make the most of your time together. Then, chapter 24, focuses on the importance of feedback with a supportive template for check-in within the appendix section. With this form, your client can reflect on the benefits of coaching they've already received and inform you what areas they still need additional support.

Next, the feedback form + testimonial request helps you capture reviews to support SEO, new client referrals and builds your public and social presence. To conclude the book, we'll run through, "Coaching Close Out Qs" as an essential practice to help your client reflect on goals, track their goal progress from the first session to current date (ie. on a scale of 1-10) and celebrate their successes. It also gives you the opportunity to provide them with an option to further their coaching journey with you, to continue growing and succeeding.

23

Starting Your Coaching Sessions

The pre-session form is a set of questions to help your client reflect on their week, what they want to get out of the next coaching session, actions they took since your last session and wins & challenges they had throughout the week. This form will also gauge experiences or emotions they have that you can discuss deeper during your next session. The responses in the pre-session form will help you prepare for the coaching session and optimize the time you have together.

Share the form up to 48 hours before the coaching session to have sufficient time to read through their answers and also help support their follow-through. Note the amount of time it takes to complete (~10 minutes) and give them a deadline to return the form. Remember, use this as a starting point to launch into a successful and meaningful coaching session.

Toussi's Top Takeaways:

- You will always have those clients that are harder to open up, the pre-session questions are a smart tool to get them talking.
- These questions help set the agenda of areas the client wants to address in the meeting.
- The pre-session form helps the client think of their wins and reminds them how great it is to have an accountability partner like you!
- The questions give your client an opportunity to reflect and begin the self-care practice of journaling.
- Store your client's weekly forms in a shared folder so you can track their goals and measure progress over time.

Appendix X - Pre-Session Form

24

How Feedback Can Help Your Business Grow

As a new coach, you're excited to get started with clients but may wonder if you're doing a good job or not. You want to be the best coach you can be for your clients. The only way to know how you're doing is by asking the client for feedback; a topic not always included in coach training and one of the things that many new coaches struggle with, but one that is ultimately essential to the growth of your business.

Checking in helps your client feel supported and learn that you are a person they can turn to when they are in need. It helps your client build a sense of being "in it together." It both checks in on progress so far and allows for adjustment of direction as necessary.

The check-in form tool in Appendix Y is a list of 5-10 questions to help you and your client reflect on the benefits of coaching thus far and areas of improvement for future sessions.

Send the form halfway into your coaching package and request they share it back with you before your next session. Be sure to review their responses together during your next session.

Toussi's Top Takeaways:

- Just before your halfway point session, tell your client you will be sharing a feedback form in an email.
- Create the check-in form on google forms so that you can collect data and store all information in one space.
- Give them a deadline to return the feedback form. Ideally this should be the next time you meet since it's now halfway into your program. Alternatively, if you choose to work with them session per session, send this after four to six sessions with the client.
- Make sure to address their feedback in the beginning of the next session; this gives your client the opportunity to expand on a point they made or share something that may have been missed.
- Timely feedback is incredibly important. Don't wait to send this!
- Many times, coaches fear feedback because it instigates feelings of judgment. But remember, it's just information that feeds learning and development. The sooner you know, the sooner you can adjust to support your client.

Appendix Y - Check-In Form

25

Last Session? How to Get Your Client Coming Back for More

A coaching feedback form is used to evaluate your client's progress and improvements to be made. Different from the check-in form, the feedback form in Appendix Z should be sent at the end of the coaching program. You've now worked together for a meaningful duration and you want your client to give you feedback on what's been the most valuable, memorable, where you shine, whether they'd refer you to a friend… and of course areas for improvement.

This should be sent to the client two sessions prior to the final session so there's sufficient time to review and ensure the client gets it to you on time. Tip?: Share the feedback form along with the testimonial request so your client has time to reflect on wins before writing their review.

Toussi's Top Takeaways:

- Use Google forms to create a feedback questionnaire. This way you can collect data and store all client information in one place. In three years time, when you've worked with 100+ clients, you'll be thanking me for this tip!
- Give your client a deadline to return the feedback form. Usually before the next time you meet (7-14 days) is more than sufficient time to fill out the form.
- Make sure to address your client feedback on what they found most rewarding in the final session reflection so you can pitch working together in the next phase of coaching.

Appendix Z - Feedback Form

26

Get that Testimonial!

A testimonial is an essential element of content marketing. Testimonials are sales tools, but more than that, they provide social proof. They are used to showcase your company's work and its reputation. You should be using testimonials to help establish credibility in the space.

Testimonials work because they aren't strong sales pitches, they come across in an unbiased voice and establish trust. You're using real people to show success in your product or service.

The email template in the appendix includes both a request for a testimonial and feedback from your coaching sessions. Bonus: it includes an incentive to further expand your clientele and branding too!

.Toussi's Top Takeaways:

- Share a deadline for the testimonial request - usually one week is sufficient timing.
- In your email request, mention how you've enjoyed working with your client and share specific and measurable progress they've made.

- Give them an incentive to write a review! Offer the gift of a session to someone in their life or a session for them to use within six months of your final coaching date.
- Insert all the channels you want them to leave a review - the most important goes first.
- Many times your client only places the review in one of the social channels you've requested. In this case, place your most important link at the top of the list. I recommend listing your google business page as this has quite a high SEO ranking.
- It's been two weeks but you still haven't received a testimonial? Write the review on their behalf in an email. State, "Writing reviews can be hard, so I wrote this on your behalf. Let me know if I can use this or you'd like to edit?" This is where you send them an example of a review and ask them to use this to edit or if they wouldn't mind pasting the example in your social channels.

Appendix Z.A - Testimonial Request

27

Finish Strong

You've reached the final session with your client! Congrats on all the support and effort you've given them. Sometimes I find that coaches get really nervous during the final coaching session, but it's important to use this as a space to remind your client of their accomplishments within the last few months.

Use the final coaching session to reflect on goals, track their goal progress from the first session to current date (ie. on a scale of 1-10), celebrate the successes and ask them to envision goals for the next year.

Remember, your client's success gives you an opportunity to take note of their results from your coaching (metrics to share with new clients, promote on your website and feel a sense of professional validation) as well as gaining knowledge to pitch the next steps of coaching together.

Ask them about their next set of goals, whether that's to close out the year or build off of what you've already worked on, and then pitch the next steps of coaching together.

Toussi's Top Takeaways:

- Closing questions help your client identify their main takeaways and what they will continue to implement after coaching with you.
- It helps the client restate the reframes they've adopted and empowers their new belief system based on the work you've done together.
- This gives you an opportunity to take note of the successes to share on your website, with new clients and in marketing content.
- Make sure to carve out 10 minutes at the end of the session to ask them about their vision for the year and address the next phase of your work together.

Appendix Z.B - Coaching Closing Questions

Closing Thoughts

Throughout this book, we've gone through the initial business concept, to closing out your last session. We've talked about what you need and don't need when setting up your online coaching business. How to define your ideal client and ensure you're drawing in the best environment. We've talked about how to set up a coaching program to help attract more success stories. And creating your social media plan, on-boarding best practices as well as how to keep clients coming back for more.

It's a lot to take in. A lot. And you still may have questions. You may even be overwhelmed. Doubts may creep in. You're most likely feeling butterflies and wondering what the f*ck you're even doing. It's completely normal. And know that there is going to be a learning curve.

Remember, this is a practical, actionable guide you can come back to time and time again. It includes specific tools, templates, structures and techniques to get from point A, all the way to point Z in your business.

You don't have to do everything at once. Take it one step at a time. Set goals and schedule internal deadlines. It's going to feel like you have a ton to do right now, so remember to celebrate the small successes and the little to-do's because when there's too much you need to do, when you're so focused on what you need to *still* get done, you will forget all the things you have done. Celebrate your wins daily!

I wrote this book because I truly wish I had these tools when I first started my business. It would have saved me time, energy and thousands of dollars. I want to help you get there. This is a guidebook to use these concepts whenever and wherever you are in your business.

At last, to end with a quote by a student of Warren G. Tracy, "Entrepreneurship is living a few years of your life like most people won't, so you can spend the rest of your life like most people can't."

Cheers to you, success coach,
Sami

Appendix A- Business Canvas

BUSINESS CANVAS

INSTRUCTION AND STEP BY STEP GUIDE

The Business Canvas is the first foundational tool to define and communicate your business idea. It is a one page document which works through the fundamental elements of your business, structuring your ideas in a coherent way to help support the vision of what's to come next.

CUSTOMER SEGMENTS

Step 1: Make sure this is specific and actionable. Focus on just one customer segment here to start. Note: You will not be losing out on clients if you don't .

EARLY ADOPTERS

Step 2: The easiest path to your customer segment. Note: If you can't get them to buy your product, it'll be harder to get others.

PROBLEM

Step 3: Identify the top three pain points for your customer segment. Why do they need your product/service?

EXISTING ALTERNATIVES

Step 4: How is this problem being solved now?

COST STRUCTURE

Step 12: Estimate your runway to get started. What are some of the initial expenses you will have?

SOLUTIONS

Step 6: Describe how you would solve these top three problems with solutions.

HIGH LEVEL CONCEPT

Step 8: Single statement to describe your idea. i.e. Youtube=Flickr for videos

UNIQUE VALUE PROPOSITION

Step 7: Represents a promise you make to your customers to get noticed. Craft this around your top problem and finished story benefit.

KEY METRICS

Step 9: What's your minimum success criteria? Keep this 3 years or less.

REVENUE STREAMS

Step 11: Start thinking about revenue sources to come up with a rough pricing model.

UNFAIR ADVANTAGE

Step 5: Something that can't easily be bought or copied. What are your strengths?

CHANNELS

Step 10: What are some paths to getting your customers to adopt your product/service?

BUSINESS CANVAS

EXAMPLE

CUSTOMER SEGMENTS

- Parents
- Family

EARLY ADOPTERS

- Moms with young kids

PROBLEM

- Parents sharing lots of photos and videos is time consuming.
- Parents have no free time.
- Families don't have the space to take nice photos and videos.

EXISTING ALTERNATIVES

- Flickr
- Facebook
- Email

COST STRUCTURE

Hosting costs –
People costs – 40 hrs *65/hr – $10K/mo

SOLUTIONS

- Instant, no upload sharing
- Integration with popular tools like iPhoto and folders.
- Automatic notification of new updates.

HIGH LEVEL CONCEPT

Photo and video sharing without uploading.

UNIQUE VALUE PROPOSITION

- Get back to the more important things in your life. Faster.
- Share your entire photo and video library under 5 minutes.

KEY METRICS

$5M/year revenue in 3 years

REVENUE STREAMS

30 day free trial, then $49/yr

UNFAIR ADVANTAGE

Personal contact list

CHANNELS

- Friends
- Daycare
- Birthday parties
- Facebook
- Google Ads
- Instagram
- Media outlets
- Word of mouth

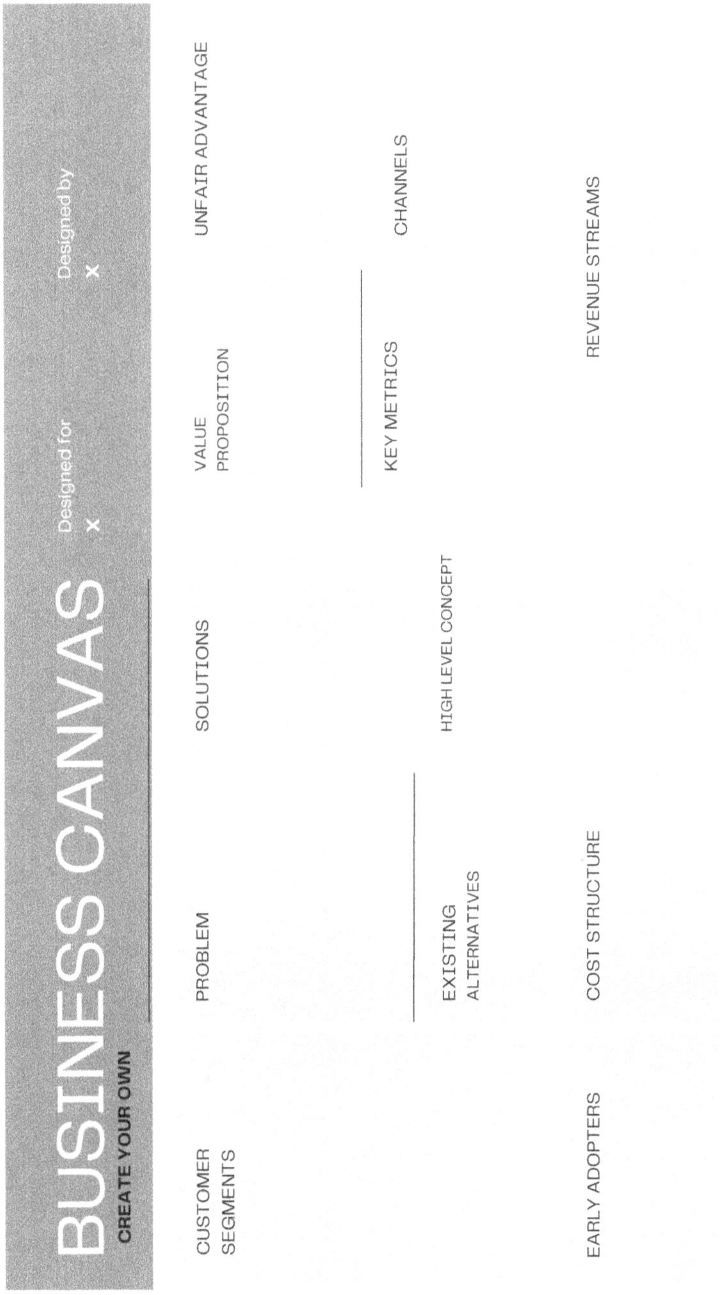

BUSINESS CANVAS

CREATE YOUR OWN

Designed for
x

Designed by
x

CUSTOMER SEGMENTS

PROBLEM

SOLUTIONS

VALUE PROPOSITION

UNFAIR ADVANTAGE

EXISTING ALTERNATIVES

HIGH LEVEL CONCEPT

KEY METRICS

CHANNELS

EARLY ADOPTERS

COST STRUCTURE

REVENUE STREAMS

Appendix B - Ideal Client Questionnaire

Having a niche is key. You may argue that this narrows your market and the number of suitable clients, but what it actually does is enable you to appeal to an audience that truly values what you do. The more you come to know your ideal client, the easier it will be for you to create content that speaks directly to them. When a potential client feels like you "get them," your offer becomes so much more appealing. Below are some categories to best identify your ideal customer. By getting to understand their values, strengths, points of consumption of your ideal customer - will help support you in targeting the growth of your company.

Type	Ideal Customer
Name	
Gender	
Age	
Enneagram	
Personality traits?	
Occupation	
Marital Status	
Location	
What do they value?	
Who are they NOT?	
What are their strengths?	
Biggest point of anxiety?	
Consumer behaviors (online? offline?)	

Where do they shop? What do they spend money on?	
Yearly income?	
What's their yearly budget?	
What media do they consume?	
What podcasts do they listen to?	
What books do they read?	
What blogs do they read?	
Who do they follow on IG/Facebook?	
What would give me credibility/authority in their eyes?	

Ideal Client Questionnaire: Example

Having a niche is key. You may argue that this narrows your market and the number of suitable clients, but what it actually does is enable you to appeal to an audience that truly values what you do. The more you come to know your ideal client, the easier it will be for you to create content that speaks directly to them. When a potential client feels like you "get them," your offer becomes so much more appealing. Below are some categories to best identify your ideal customer. By getting to understand their values, strengths, points of consumption of your ideal customer - will help support you in targeting the growth of your company.

Type	Ideal Customer
Name	Rachel
Gender	Female
Age	33
Enneagram	Type 3
Personality traits?	Uneasy, doubtful, lonely, stressed, resentful
Occupation	Consultant
Marital Status	Single
Location	Los Angeles
What do they value?	Family, professional status, relationships, freedom, independence
Who are they NOT?	Confident, happy, fulfilled, secure, purposeful
What are their strengths?	Ambition, outgoing, intelligence

Biggest point of anxiety?	Loss of identity and sense of self, confidence in job, challenging relationship with dating, hates 9-5 and wants to start a business
Consumer behaviors (online? offline?)	80% online shopper / 20% offline shopper
Where do they shop? What do they spend money on?	Lululemon, Zara, Revolve, Saks Fifth Avenue; clothes, accessories
Yearly income?	$150,000
What's their yearly budget?	$10,000 per year
What media do they consume?	Instagram & Facebook
What podcasts do they listen to?	Professional growth, Love podcasts
What books do they read?	Sel-help books
What blogs do they read?	NA
Who do they follow on IG/ Facebook?	@CreativeCultivate, @ MarieForleo, @Deepak-Chopra, FB: Single Ladies in Los Angeles
What would give me credibility/authority in their eyes?	Launched successful business 5 years of coaching training 10,000+ hours coaching high-acheivers Owned matchmaking company 10+ years experience with management

Appendix C - Unique Selling Proposition (USP)

Before you can begin selling your product or service to anyone else, you have to sell yourself on it. This is especially important when your service is similar to others. Very few businesses are one-of-a-kind. Just look around you: How many consultants, coaches, therapists, healers, physicians and other service based companies are out there? How many are truly unique?

The key to effective selling in this situation is what advertising and marketing professionals call a "unique selling proposition" (USP). Unless you can pinpoint what makes your business unique in a world of homogeneous competitors, you cannot target your sales efforts successfully.

Pinpointing your USP requires some hard soul-searching and creativity. One way to start is to analyze how other companies use their USP's to their advantage. This requires careful analysis of other companies' ads and marketing messages. If you analyze what they say they sell, not just their product or service characteristics, you can learn a great deal about how companies distinguish themselves from competitors.

The USP is also often the first bit of copy you'll see above the fold on a given company's homepage. It's typically a single sentence-length headline, and is sometimes accompanied by a sub-headline. The essential word in the phrase is "unique." The USP defines your position in the market insofar as it answers the question: What's the ultimate point of differentiation between you and your competitors that makes your company the one worth doing business with?

Before you start thinking about which qualities set your business apart from similar companies, you need to know almost everything about your perfect customer.

When you're identifying your ideal prospect, consider the following:

- *What does your perfect customer really want?*
- *How can your product or service solve their problem(s)?*
- *What factors motivate their buying decisions?*
- *Why do your existing customers choose your business over your competitors?*

Remember – it's not enough to merely target a rough demographic. You need to know exactly who you want to sell to and why. Once you know this, you can get to work on the next unique selling proposition best practice, which is...

Consumers don't want to buy products – they want to solve their problems. This could be as simple as purchasing a reliable set of tools that will last for years, but it can (and frequently is) much more complex.

Take the cosmetics industry, for example. Companies in this space don't just sell make-up – they sell lifestyle ideals; glamor, confidence and style. Think about this in a problem-solving context; people who may not feel glamorous, confident or stylish will if they use a particular product. This lies at the heart of most cosmetics advertising, and this concept applies to many other industries too.

To create a strong USP, you have to examine the profile of your perfect customer and then market your products in a way that shows them you can meet their needs and solve their problems. You can't hope to write persuasive, compelling copy in the voice of the customer unless you know who they are. If your prospective customers choose your products, how will their lives be improved? What makes your business so different that prospective customers should choose your products or services?

The answers to these questions should form the bedrock of your USP.

Formula: End Result Customer Wants + Specific Period of Time + Address the Objections

USP Examples:

1. Hot fresh pizza delivered to your door in 30 minutes or it's free. (Dominos)
2. FedEx's slogan of "When it absolutely, positively has to be there overnight"
3. Vistaprint is a one-stop shop for online printing: You can order everything you need online and get it shipped fast.
4. Voodoo Doughnut's Unique Selling Proposition: Donuts So Wacky, the Wait Is Part of the Experience
5. Death Wish Coffee: A lot of coffee shops and roasters lay claim to having the "smoothest" or "richest" cup of coffee out there. Death Wish Coffee, however, chose to cater to those who need an extra kick in their cup of joe by instead selling the, "world's strongest coffee".

Step 1:

Braindump three ideas for your USP.

1. ____
2. ____
3. ____

Step 2:

Now ask yourself:

- Is your USP around your top problem and finished story benefit?
- Did you avoid empty buzz words?
- Is it under 140 characters?
- Are you being specific?

Step 3:

Choose one USP to practice out loud and test with friends.

Note: Continue refining if needed.

Appendix D - Business Questionnaire

At this point, you've completed your lean canvas and are ready to move into more detail about your who, what and why of your business. Don't worry, though, there are no "right answers." So even if you haven't done everything you want to or haven't even started, view this as an opportunity to begin brainstorming. Please answer what you can to use as a jumping off point for further ideation and execution. You can use this to set up attainable marketing/business development goals and action items for yourself moving forward. The more information you share, the more thorough you can be in months to come.

1. Describe your company/what you do in a paragraph.
2. When you meet people (e.g. at a party), how do you briefly describe what you do?
3. What is the story *behind* your company? Why were you inspired to create it or do this?
4. Are there ever pleasant surprises for clients once they start working with you? What didn't they expect? Check out testimonials or review feedback forms as a reflection tool.
5. On the flipside: are there ever misunderstandings about what you do (or don't do) that you wish people understood better?
6. What do you think other businesses are missing? What is the industry failing to offer its clients right now?
7. What are your biggest marketing goals? *(e.g. "raising awareness that my business exists," "retaining current clients and getting more business from them," "brand building").*

8. As you consider the future of your business, *what does success look like for you?*

9. Who is or who will be your target market? How did you decide this?

10. Is this market typically aware that they need someone like you?

11. What's the turning point where you think clients will tend to come running your way? What will be going on for them that makes them reach out to someone like you?

12. Do you have any insight into how clients make their decisions about engaging services like yours? What do you think tends to make/break their decision to go with you, specifically?

13. Who do you consider to be your main competitors? Please give 2-4 names and websites (if possible). *For each, please be as detailed as possible about why you feel you're different, and why that matters for a client.*

14. How are you positioned in the market right now? Or how do you want to be positioned? (e.g. "the go-to new mom's coach").

15. What do you believe will be your biggest marketing challenges going forward? (e.g. resources/personnel, budget, competition, etc.).

16. What do you *worry* about most when it comes to marketing your business? (e.g. social media, networking with potential clients, partnerships)

17. What marketing materials are you currently using or want to use? (e.g. website, brochures, introductory letters, personal pitches, business cards, website, social media, etc.).

18. Now that you read that list, are there specific materials you wish you had?

19. For marketing materials you use or want to use, how will you monitor their success?

20. How often do you interact with your key *existing* clients?

21. Where do you interact with them?

22. Are there opportunities for your clients to offer feedback about your work, for example a follow-up survey? If so, have you written this out or what are you hearing from them?

23. If you had to *guess*, what do you think your clients would criticize/suggest you improve, if pushed to make a comment? If you don't have this, leave it blank.

24. Although it's early on in your business, are there any success stories with clients that you're proud of?

25. What types of clients do you most enjoy working with? What types of clients do you "click" with the most? Why do you think that is?

26. Are you aware of your/your company's online reputation? (Have you ever Googled it?) Is it consistent with the brand you want to create?

27. I've already asked you to write about your primary target market. Is there *any other (secondary)* market that you feel might benefit from what you do? What is it, and why do you think it's a potential fit?

28. What are the *top 3* things you want prospective clients to know & remember about your company?
    1.
    2.
    3.

29. Are people (colleagues, partner, family, etc.) aware of your company's brand and marketing message? How would they describe you?

30. Do you have or want to have a blog or a newsletter? Do you enjoy this type of writing?

31. What types of content are you most interested in developing? Written? Video? Social media?

32. When it comes to marketing tasks, which do you find *least* painful to do?(!) – or: what are you most interested in trying out?

33. What topics do you want to or currently write/post about?

34. What topics might your clients want to hear about regularly? What are their ongoing concerns?

35. If you use social media (including Twitter, Instagram, LinkedIn, Facebook), do you regularly monitor and respond to outside conversations and your followers' comments and questions? How frequently do you engage (react/respond to others)?

36. Please note any certifications, awards or involvements you have, particularly any that might make you stand apart to a potential client.

37. If there are any important dates in your industry (e.g. "National XXXX Month", etc.) to use in your marketing strategy, please list them here:

38. Do you participate in any customer-facing events where you could promote your business? What organizations are you a member of?

39. What accomplishment(s) are you most proud of with relation to your work so far? Or what do you see accomplishing in the future?

40. What are some keywords you use when thinking about your business?

Appendix E - Client & Competitive Unfair Advantage Guide

The Client & Competitive Unfair Advantage Guide will help you build trust and credibility with clients and prospective clients. Follow the steps below to find a picture of your ideal client, answer questions on the current or potential trust of your client and learn how to draft a short bio about your work to increase confidence in your business.

See below steps on both the guide and examples to support your success in building out this guide.

Step 1:

Find an image of your ideal client.

Step 2:

Answer Qs below to better understand your unfair advantage:

What are your clients' top three challenges?

1. _______________________________________
2. _______________________________________
3. _______________________________________

Why does your ideal client trust you to support her?

-
-
-
-
-

Past experiences and accomplishments that help your ideal client trust you:

-
-
-
-
-

Future experiences that will help your ideal client trust you:

-
-
-
-

Keywords on what the business will visually communicate:

-
-
-
-
-

Step 3:

Business Owner Bio Draft

Learning how to write a bio is not easy; defining yourself in a few words even less so. But never fear—you **can** do it! You'll probably want to write a mid-length description of both your current role, professional aspirations, and biggest achievements. Professional bios allow you to go into a bit more detail—so here we go! Remember, you'll want to include your name, company, goals and aspirations, 2-3 most impressive and relevant achievements and quirky fact about you (if it's appropriate to the site).

Coach Bio Draft

____

____

____

____

____

____

EXAMPLE: Client Avatar & Unfair Advantage Guide

Step 1:

Find an image of your ideal client.

Step 2:

Answer Qs below to better understand your unfair advantage:

What are your clients' top three challenges?

- Perfectionism
- People Pleasing
- Over scheduling/burnout

Why does your ideal client trust you to support her?

- **Experience: I have moved through these challenges myself.**
- I have made clear that I understand her challenges and her motivations to get through them.
- Proven and tested to work: I **practice what I preach.**
- Provide a no-judgment zone and I'm an active listener: I'm easy to talk to.

Past experiences and accomplishments that help your ideal client trust you:

- Moving myself from burnout in a career that wasn't for me into my dream career.
- Happiness certified training in life coaching.
- Positive reviews from clients that I've helped in the past.
- Multifaceted experience: Living in different cities, holding several different jobs to give me a diverse understanding of people from different walks of life.

Future experiences that will help your ideal client trust you:

- Experience working with clients on burnout recovery, self-care and mental health.
- More testimonials/positive reviews from previous clients.
- Written publications in outlets she likes.
- Writing my own book!

Keywords on what the business will visually communicate:

- PEACE
- ACCEPTANCE
- GROWTH
- AUTHENTICITY
- SELF-COMPASSION

Step 3:

Business Owner Bio Draft

Sami Toussi, Board Certified Coach (BCC), is a career strategist and owner of Toussi International, a consultancy that helps individuals tap into their purpose to benefit the world. Toussi's business encompasses more than 10 years of business and psychology experience, where she earned over six figures by her mid-twenties leading an international sales team. Despite Toussi's early success her experience caused her to question the fullness and purpose of her life. Seeking answers, Toussi further delved into the coaching world and gained board certification in 2016. Toussi then founded Toussi International, a global consulting practice with clients ranging from business owners to professionals to multinational corporations.

Appendix F - Coaching Program

A coaching program is key to create long-lasting results for your ideal client and for you! It also moves you from being a "freelancer" to an "entreprenuer." Why? Programs help you attract more success stories, because you are working with a client for a longer period of time to reach a specific goal, such as building their email list, creating a coaching program, or becoming more attractive to their ideal partner. A program helps clients to have a clearer idea of what they can expect to accomplish through your work together. It can also increase their confidence in your ability to help them get the results you promise. Below answer the questions to help provoke thoughts and ideas abou the phase, reflection point, material, and added value of how your program will best support your client in getting the results they need to attain success.

Class Session	Session Title	Phase in Process	Content	Reflection	Material	Benefits for Clients
Session No.	What title best explains the results of this session?	Name the step of the program so both you and client knows the step of the program(i.e. Clarity, Awareness, Vision, Goal-Setting)	What content will be covered in the session?	What does the client need to think about in order to get the most out of this time together?	What materials or tools will support the client get to the results they need within the session?	How will this session support your client's problems? Reflect back on their pain points. In what ways does this support the client in feeling like they are making progress/improving their life?

1	Introduction	Clarity	Course Introduction, Wheel of Life Review, Goal Defining	Why am I here? What do I want from this program?	Time management strategy template Wheel of Life Review Reflection & Intentions worksheet	-Increased self-awareness -Support and plan to take next steps -Accountability

Appendix G - Website Outline

A website outline is used to prepare content for every page of your website. The homepage should include at minimum: 1. Intro (your unique value proposition, above the fold) 2. Services, 3. About Me, 4. Contact button. Other pages on the website can include your testimonials, blogs, a longer "about me" section and additional resources you want your prospective clients to see. Use the website outline below to keep all key material well-organized before creating your website. Note: both the instructions and examples are outlined to support your success.

HOMEPAGE:

1- Intro (homepage)
[Insert unique value proposition]
I help **(insert who)**... break free from **(insert what)** and live with **(insert result)**

2- Pain Points
If you are...
Identify their top three pain points such as:
-An entrepreneur feeling stuck, ineffective and disconnected from purpose
-An new leader struggling to manage their time and support their teams
-A burned out people pleaser in need of rest & relaxation to lead a balanced lifestyle
...you're in the right place.

2a- Services
[List service offerings below]
Career Coaching

Group Program
One-On-One Program

Leadership
One-On-One Program

Confidence Coaching
One-On-One Program

3- About Me
I'm a X, X, X with three intersecting areas of passion and expertise:

- Insert your passions and expertise
- Write about why your client should trust you

> ABOUT ME
> Call to Action (CTA) button

4- Schedule a Consult
[Include a call to action button]

To explore the possibility of us working together, please schedule a free 30-minute consultation call.

> SCHEDULE A CALL
> Call to Action (CTA) button

PAGE 1:

About Me/My Business

The mission of my business, **(insert name of business)**, is to help people... **(insert mission statement)** break free from... and live and work with....

Why trust you?/My work is guided by five core values:
[List the five points you made within your unfair advantage questionnaire and 3-5 fun facts or stats about you]

PAGE 2:

Testimonials

[List any testimonials you have on this page]

```
SCHEDULE A CALL
Call to Action (CTA) button
```

PAGE 3:

Blogs

Year 1: Include one blog per quarter per your business theme
Year 2-3: Try for one blog per month. This will support the SEO
of your site.

```
SCHEDULE A CALL
Call to Action (CTA) button
```

PAGE 4:

Consult: Call to Action
Schedule a Consult

To explore the possibility of us working together, please
schedule a free 30-minute consultation call. Make sure this
page leads to your schedule using platforms like Calendly or
Acuity so it's easy for them to sign up for a consultation!

The consultation is an opportunity for us to get to know your
goals **(enlist how you help them)** in order **(list result you
provide)**.

```
SCHEDULE A CALL
Call to Action (CTA) button
```

Appendix H - Search Engine Optimization: Guide

How to Grow Your Website Traffic

Did you know there are 3.5 Billion searches on Google a day? SEO stands for Search Engine Optimization which is the process of optimizing your website to get free traffic from search engines like Google. To get started, first, make sure that your search engine knows what your website is all about. Find relevant keywords that people are searching for by putting yourself in the shoes of a potential customer. Below are four areas to reflect on in order to increase website traffic and grow your coaching practice.

1- Service Phrase

Over the last 18 years, as the coaching profession grew, the number of searches around coaching shot up — terms like *life coaching* and *business coaching* increased. It's savvy to get these words into your pages but, it's even better to be specific and differentiate yourself....

Here are more service phrases examples:

- BUSINESS PLANNING
- CAREER COUNSELING
- DATING ADVICE
- ONLINE TRAINING

- COACHING BUSINESS
- BUSINESS GROWTH
- JOB SEARCH
- CAREER ADVISOR
- BUSINESS MENTOR
- EXECUTIVE COACH.

2- User Pain Points

Know your user pain points to address their challenges in the content of your marketing. This will help your audience feel "seen and heard." Pain point examples can include:

- HOW DO I QUIT SMOKING
- HOW DO I LOSE WEIGHT FAST
- SHOULD I DIVORCE MY WIFE
- COMMON CAUSES OF FATIGUE IN MEN
- FINDING A NEW CAREER AT 50.
- HOW TO LEAD A TEAM MEETING

3- Blog Titles

Blogs titles should focus on solutions to support your clients. Writing content will be easy if you approach it this way - what are some of the blogs I need to attract my customer? Remember, blogs build your credibility as a talented coach and search engines love sending traffic to blogs. Examples may include:

- BECOME PROFITABLE
- FIND LOVE AFTER DIVORCE
- RETIRE HAPPY
- 5-STEPS TO MAKE 1K PER DAY.

4- Your Coaching Title

The number of searches for phrases such as *life coach, health coach* and *relationship coach* has also grown.

Use them throughout your website content, especially when referring to yourself, like on your About Me page.

Also, consider similar terms that people use like *executive coach, business mentor, nutritionist* and *career advisor*.

It's all about great keyword phrases. For coaches, the seven sources I recommend are:

1. SERVICE PHRASES
2. YOUR COACHING TITLE
3. PAIN POINTS
4. DESIRED OUTCOMES
5. YOUR NAME
6. JARGON & BUZZ WORDS
7. YOUR LOCATION.

Miscellaneous Notes

Check out google trends to identify where people are searching for coaches: https://trends.google.com/trends/explore?geo=US&q=%2Fm%2F0122dh

Think about both your On page SEO = Link Building + OFF-PAGE SEO = Get other websites to link to your pages/Quality backlinks to rank high on google through channels such as:

- Forums
- Directories
- Editorials (blog)

Appendix I - Business Email Launch

The email launch party is a big email sent to your network to share the news about your new business! Large brands use email marketing to build hype for a new launch, features, or an event. You'll be using this email template before you're fully "ready" to tell people about your business, but you should already have some sort of online presence (either website or social page). Make sure to start with a short greeting and include a powerful call to action so that it's easy for your audience to take the next step. Why is this crucial? Because we need to tell our nearest and dearest about our new business - they will be our ambassadors to grow the brand!

Re: Launching my business!

Hi Family & Friends,

As you know, I have many interests which have led me into various careers as I search for what my true passion is. Through this exploration, I realized that each field I ventured into shared the same theme. And what was that theme? Mentoring people, supporting them to solve their problems and empowering them to get to their goals. This is where I truly find happiness. I have found that I am happiest whenever I'm helping people identify and solve their problems.

Over the past few months I've been working to start my own coaching business to support people who are tired of compromising in their life. I am writing to you today because as of this morning, my website, _________, is live and I am officially taking on new clients!

I'm writing to ask two things:

1. If you know anyone who would be interested in learning more about or could benefit from the work I do, please feel free to send me their contact information or direct them to my website.
2. If I have ever given you advice that's been helpful, please consider writing a testimonial that I can use on my website/on social media. You can include your first name only or your initials, just let me know what you prefer. Please include this on the channels here (*link this to your newly created Google Business and Yelp business profiles.*)

I appreciate all of your support as I embark on this journey!

Cheers,

[Your Name]

[Website]

[LinkedIn Page]

[Instagram Page]

Appendix J - Customer Experience Workflow

Developing and refining a client workflow will ensure you follow the principles to delight your clients and overall business. An optimized workflow reduces errors, improves collaboration, acknowledges the business value and reduces time to market saving the organization time and money. See below for an example of a strong workflow form pre-onboarding, on-boarding, before sessions, in sessions and post-session guidelines to follow.

Pre-Onboarding

- [Prospective Client] signs up for consultation
- Send automated personal email
- [Prospective Client] submits intake form
  - How can I be of service?
  - What are goals that are important to you?
- Consult on either of the following:
  - Zoom video
  - Audio call
- Upon meeting probe Qs and convey the following about you:
  - Personal story
  - Service offering (i.e. program)
  - On-boarding process (timing, deliverables, pricing)

But.. What if they need time to "think about it"?

- Schedule check-in call to follow up
- Send follow up email and value-add worksheet

Onboarding

- First session scheduled through online scheduler
- [New Client] sends payment + signs contract before meeting one

Before Sessions

- **15 minutes:** Review client notes from previous session/ intake call

In Program Sessions

- **10 minutes:** Check-in
  - How are they doing?
  - What do they want to work on today
- **30 minutes:** Discussion with client around goals achieved and goals they're working towards. Will continue to bring clients back to goals.
- **10 minutes:** Wrap up
  - What we discussed
  - Goal setting for the next week
  - Check-in with how client feels and what they want to work on next time
  - Book the next session with the client if time isn't recurring.
- Send follow-up email with next session reminder & goals.

After Sessions - *Client Folder*

- Add goals and notes from session to their client folder as well as assigned homework

After Sessions - *Internal Records*

- Keep track of how many sessions they've booked/used (package)
- Update internal documents for goal setting for client
  - What goals have they been reaching?
  - What goals have they been struggling with?
  - Spend time planning next session
- Answer emails
  - Keep track of how many emails client sends per month and how much time spent

Closing Out Sessions

- Send feedback form + testimonial request 3 sessions prior to close out.
  - **Do not send this after their final session.** It doesn't give them enough incentive to share. By sharing these 3 sessions prior to close out, your client will have sufficient time, can provide strong feedback and you can hold them accountable
- Review closing questions 20 minutes during final session
- If they don't sign up for another program, schedule a check-in call within 30-90 days to see how they are doing
  - Note: A lot can change in three months so your support may be needed again. Also, if they haven't sent over a testimonial this can be your opportunity to request it again!

Bonus: Pre-OnBoarding I Workflow Templates

Use the communication platform, Calendly, as your one-stop shop for prospective clients to easily schedule "discovery calls." A discovery call is the first conversation with a prospect after they show initial interest in your product. It's your opportunity to get to know the customer to see if they could be a good fit for your business. The Customer Workflow function helps you automate the client experience. See below for scripts to ensure you create a personalized and supportive quality service before your prospect becomes a new client!

EMAIL: CONSULTATION CANCELLATION/RESCHEDULE

Email notifications will be sent to your invitee if you cancel the event.

Canceled: {{event_name}} with {{my_name}} on {{event_date}}

Hi {{Invitee_Full_Name}},

Hope you're doing well! Apologies but the Toussi International calendar wasn't updated accordingly and your {{event_name}} at {{event_time}} on {{event_date}} has been rescheduled to {{event_time}} on {{event_date}}.

Please confirm the new time works well for you!

In the meantime, feel free to look through some client success stories [link website here].

Best,

[Your name]

[Website]
[LinkedIn Page]
[Instagram Page]

TEXT REMINDER: BEFORE CONSULTATION

Reminder: {{event_name}} with {{my_name}} at {{event_time}} on {{event_date}}

See you soon! - [Your name]

EMAIL REMINDER: BEFORE CONSULTATION

An invitee will receive a reminder email before a scheduled event at specified times.

Subject: Reminder: Strategy Consultation with [your name] at 3 PM on July 27 2022

Hi {{Invitee_First_Name}},

This is a friendly reminder that your {{event_name}} with {{my_name}} is at {{event_time}} on {{event_date}}.

Location

Event Description

FAQ Link

In case you have trouble logging in, please send [your name] a message at [insert email].

Best,

[Your name]
[Website]

[LinkedIn Page]
[Instagram Page]

[Timing: 24 hours before, 8 hours before]

POST CONSULT: EMAIL FOLLOW UP

Subject: To further growth! I Consultation

Hi {{Invitee_ First_ Name}},

It was great meeting with you today!

I wanted to thank you again for opening up about your goals and sharing your journey with me.

I really connected with you and know our work together can bridge the gap between where you are now and where you want to be.

Please let me know if you have any feedback or additional requests regarding the coaching offer.

Lastly, feel free to look through client success stories [link website here]!

Best,

[Your name]
[Website]
[LinkedIn Page]
[Instagram Page]

Appendix K - Powerful Coaching Engagement Structure

As a life, career, relationship, business or spiritual coach you may be hired for helping your clients build confidence, vision, goals, or a specific area of life. Let's assume you have a client that is facing lack of confidence. Below is a guideline and checklist on how to conduct sessions to best support their growth. Use this form to check off your presence and operations before, during and after coaching sessions.

• STEP 1: Prepare the Space

0-15 minutes before the session

Spend time preparing for the session. Clear your mind and your energy and be ready to hold the space for your client. Pull any notes you may have on this client. This will prepare you for the session. Now get yourself in a state of confidence and power. You will need it to help your client.

• STEP 2: Build Rapport

0-5 minutes into the session

Acknowledge them for showing up and assure them they are in a safe place where nothing that they say will be disclosed. Check in with how they are feeling in that moment.

- ## **STEP 3: Set Vision & Goals**

5-15 minutes into the session

Dive in your client's vision for life. You can use assessments to evaluate various aspects of your client's life. Once you have helped them assess various areas of their life, ask them to pick one area of life that needs the most focus.

Once you have the area, take them through a mental journey into the future. Ask them what their ideal life will look like in that area in 1 year, or if you have a longer contract, in 3 years.

- ## **STEP 4: Coach through a Challenge**

15-40 minutes into the session

Now that they have their future envisioned, ask them what could possibly stop them from making their dreams come true? Listen for what they are saying.

Listen for what are the invisible scripts that might be the core reason for their lack of confidence and belief in themselves. For example, they may be dealing with a past belief where their capabilities were criticized by an authority figure - like a parent or teacher.

Challenge those beliefs.

Ask provocative questions that engage their rational and irrational mind to solve solutions to these potential challenges.

- **STEP 5: Commit to Action & Close on a Positive Note**

40-45 minutes into the session

Recap key points and agree on an action plan that you will hold them accountable for. Close the session on a positive note and with clarity on next steps.

- **STEP 6: Do a Post Session Follow Up**

After the session

Follow up and send any additional information that could help them.

Appendix L - Coaching Development Plan

The Coaching Development Plan (CDP) is an opportunity to set clear intentions and goals with a new client in your very first session together. When you don't set clear intentions at the start of your journey with a new client, you're opening yourself up to all kinds of trouble. It's a simple step, but when you miss it - disaster. The CDP helps your client see the magic and the results of your work together. It will help your client understand how you've been supporting them, how you've helped them in the past and how you can help them now and in the future. Setting intentions and reminding your clients of these intentions creates a container for trackable, impactful results.

WHAT'S A CDP?

A coaching engagement starts with clarity about the purpose of the coaching:

- **What**'s the vision for the coaching client, whether that's self-aspiration or in conjunction with expectations by management in a corporate setting.
- **How** does your client build relationships and engage with others in the process of fulfilling their vision?
- **Who**; what are the thoughts, beliefs, attitudes, approaches, emotional states and more, that will support the building of relationships, and move them toward their aspiration or vision.

INTENTION SETTING

Use the following questions to set practical and clear intentions:

- What are the outcomes you are expecting out of our coaching sessions?
- What is the vision for our work together here?
- Are you 100% committed to this coaching experience?
- Are you willing to NOT let your fear get in the way?

When you've discussed these questions, **note down the answers** somewhere so that you can refer to them regularly with your client. These intentions will do more than create clear expectations at the start. They will also help you track progress over the long-term, showing your clients how you've been successful in helping them achieve their goal

Setting intentions and reminding your clients of these intentions creates a container for trackable, impactful results.

SESSIONS

- Step 1: Start your sessions by reflecting on what your client wants to accomplish in one year's time. You can ask "What outcomes do you want to see in the six months of our time together?"
- Step 2: Write their goals in a shared document and take note of how satisfied they feel in accomplishing this goal from day one to day 30, 60, 90, etc.
- Step 3: Revert back to these goals at the beginning of each month to _track satisfaction rate._

The close of a coaching engagement has at least these three components, based on the CDP:

1. Review their CDP for progress
2. Celebrate successes
3. Discuss what's next.

REVIEW THEIR CDP FOR PROGRESS

Have your client formally review their CDP with you for progress made within each component of their plan (What, How, Who). Where specific measures of success were determined in advance, review for what actually occurred.

Oftentimes my client presents their progress and successes to their manager, and the manager gives their observations as well. My role is to support my client to prepare for that meeting. I, as the coach, also give my observations. I **notice their efforts, their experiments and their self-awareness.**

CELEBRATE SUCCESSES

This part is often missed. As human beings, we seem to be wired for continually looking at what's next, or what's wrong; and in the process we forget to celebrate what we just accomplished.

Celebrating involves the client reflecting on the successes they've had, as well as how they created those successes. In the process of discussing successes, the coach can ask questions to **help the client draw out what occurred,** so they can **use that information to create further success.**

DISCUSS WHAT'S NEXT

If someone is working with being more patient with others and channeling their frustration more constructively, it may take a lot of ongoing intention and effort to practice a different way of expressing emotion.

How is your coaching client going to support themselves beyond the coaching engagement? Sometimes, **it's further coaching sessions** and if in a company setting, then preparing the case for further coaching investment.

Where further coaching isn't the chosen option, then support your client to consider ways they will continue their progress. One of the best gifts we can give our clients is that of the joy of being a continuous learner. No matter how lofty we have ascended in our career or what age we are, we can always learn new things about ourselves, and others.

Appendix M - Social Media Strategy

3	IG Checklist	Ideation	QC checklist to ensure you're on the right track and incorporating your non-negotiables onto IG
4	2022 Calendar Year	Ideation	Example of social media holiday themes to support creating content
5	Calendar Example	Content Creation	An example of a social calendar month incorporating your business themes - note: 3 posts per week is sufficient
6	Monthly Plan	Content Creation	For simplicity and ease of automation, create a theme for each month of the year, list out your reasoning for the monthly theme and brainstorm ideas for social posts.

7	Possible Partnerships	Future Strategy	Ready to connect with complimentary businesses to support your growth? Identify the name of the business, whether you have an existing relationship, their website, product, IG handle, all the things to begin connecting.

BUSINESS THEMES

Your (Brand) Voice	Examples	Create Your Own
Brand Voice represents your brand's unique perspective and the values you stand for. In other words, this is your brand's overall personality. Your tone of voice refers to how your brand communicates with your audience, which can include word choice, communication style, and emotional tone.	Formal, informal, humorous, optimistic, assertive, thoughtful, respectful...	

Your (Brand) Appearance	Examples	Create Your Own
Brand personality is a framework that helps a company or organization shape the way people feel about its product, service, or mission. A company's brand personality elicits an emotional response in a specific consumer segment, with the intention of inciting	Luxury brands, such as Michael Kors and Chanel, aim for sophistication by focusing on an upper-class, glamorous, and trendy lifestyle, which attracts a high-spending consumer base. Examples include: Excitement: Carefree, spirited, and youthful	

positive actions that benefit the firm. Customers are more likely to purchase a brand if its personality is similar to their own.	Sincerity: Kindness, thoughtfulness, and an orientation toward family values Ruggedness: Rough, tough, outdoorsy, and athletic Competence: Successful, accomplished, and influential, which is highlighted by leadership Sophistication: Elegant, prestigious, and sometimes even pretentious	
Your (Brand) Colors	**Examples**	**Create Your Own**
Palette of around two to three colors that are used to represent your company. A consistent and strategic application of brand colors can increase brand awareness and recognizability. Colour sets the mood of brand expression. Emotions are powerful and have the ability to drive decision	Blues & Neutrals	

making. Brands want to cultivate strong emotional connections with their customers and this can't be done with just a logo; colours are needed to cultivate these emotions.		

Themes of Your Business	Post Ideas	Create Your Own
Time Management & Organization	Tips/Plans	
Relationships & Boundaries	Personal/Client Stories	
Leadership Style & Skillset	Educational	
Career Growth / Management Growth	Stories/Educational	
Finding Flow/ Balance	Reflections/Stories	
Authentically You	Client Stories	
Mind-Body Connection	Educational	
Communication	Stories/Examples	
Goal Setting to Actionable Plans	Educational/ Examples	
High Performance Teams	Stories	

Personal Interests	Post Ideas	Create Your Own
Family & Friends	Personal Experiences	
Local Businesses - Restaurants/Bars	Personal Photos	
Mountains	Resources	
Travel	Future Plans	
My Personal Flow/ Balance	Personal Experiences	

CLIENT AVATAR

Gender	
Age	
What's their personality?	
What do they value?	
Who are they NOT?	
What are their strengths?	
Biggest point of anxiety?	
Consumer behaviors	
What are their consumer behaviors? What do they spend money on?	
What's their income?	
What SM do they consume?	
What podcasts do they listen to?	
What books do they read?	
What blogs do they read?	
What magazines do they read?	
Who do they follow on IG?	

What would give me credibility/authority in their eyes?	
Brand partnerships	
Certifications/qualifications	
Data to share	
Media features	

3 Biggest Problems	
3 Solutions	
Piece from Bio	

INSTAGRAM CHECKLIST (EXAMPLE)

Activity	Y/N
Using Social Media Holidays to create posts	
3 posts per week	
1 call to action per week	
1 reel per month	
Quotes on business/time management/balance	
Small business, Hiring well, Marketing strategies, Brand building questionnaire, Pricing, Unique Value Proposition, Time management, Balance, Priorities	
1 graph per month	
Promote 1 client testimonial per month	
Promote 1 client page per month	

Use stories feature 2x per week *share inspiring quotes*	
Incorporate monthly themes into posts	
Ensure all hashtags are included	

SOCIAL MEDIA HOLIDAYS

SOCIAL MEDIA HOLIDAYS

Important Holidays

INSENSE

January

01 New Year's Day
02 Science Fiction Day
04 Trivia Day
06 National Technology Day
10 National Cut Your Energy
    Costs Day
    Clean Off Your Desk Day
20 Cheese Lovers Day
21 National Hugging Day
24 National Compliment Day
31 Inspire Your Heart with Art Day

February

01 Chinese New Year
04 World Cancer Day
07 National Send a Card to
    a Friend Day
09 National Pizza Day
14 Valentine's Day
15 Family Day
16 National Pancake Day
17 Random Acts of Kindness Day
20 Love Your Pet Day
21 International Mother Language
    Day

March

03 World Wildlife Day
04 National Employee
    Appreciation Day
    National Day of Unplugging
08 International Women's Day
10 Popcorn Lover's Day
    #PopcornLoversDay
17 St. Patrick's Day
19 National Let's Laugh Day
20 International Day of Happiness
21 World Poetry Day
31 Transgender Day of Visibility

April

01 April Fools Day
03 Find a Rainbow Day
06 National Walking Day
10 National Siblings Day
16 National Stress Awareness Day
22 Earth Day
23 National Picnic Day
    World Book Day
29 International Dance Day
30 National Honesty Day

May

01 International Workers Day
04 Star Wars Day
06 National Nurses Day
08 Mother's Day
16 Love a Tree Day
17 Day Against Homophobia
    & Transphobia
21 National Bike to Work Day
24 National Scavenger Hunt Day
30 National Creativity Day

June

02 Leave The Office Early Day
04 National Donut Day
08 World Oceans Day
    Best Friends Day
13 International Children's Day
20 First Day of Summer
    Father's Day
21 World Music Day
    National Selfie Day
25 Take Your Dog to Work Day
27 National PTSD Awareness Day

July

04 Independence Day
07 World Chocolate Day
15 Give Something Away Day
17 World Emoji Day
18 National Ice Cream Day
25 Parents' Day
26 Disability Independence Day
30 Talk in an Elevator Day

August

02 National Coloring Book Day
08 International Cat Day
09 National Book Lovers Day
12 International Youth Day
16 National Tell A Joke Day
19 World Photo Day
26 Women's Equality Day
    National Dog Day

September

05 International Day Of Charity
09 Stand Up To Cancer Day
21 International Day Of Peace
22 Car-Free Day
    Fall Begins
27 World Tourism Day

October

01 National Coffee Day
    World Vegetarian Day
02 International Day of
    Nonviolence
04 National Taco Day
10 World Mental Health Day
14 World Sight Day
17 International Day for the
    Eradication of Poverty
30 Checklist Day
31 Hallowe'en

November

01 World Vegan Day
03 National Sandwich Day
04 National Candy Day
13 World Kindness Day
16 National Entrepreneurs Day
24 Thanksgiving Day
25 Black Friday
28 Cyber Monday

December

01 World AIDS Day
03 International Day of Persons
    with Disabilities
04 National Cookie Day
10 Human Rights Day
18 Hanukkah begins
21 Crossword Puzzle Day
    First Day of Winter
25 Christmas Day
31 New Year's Eve

POSSIBLE PARTNERSHIPS

Name	Business	Relationship	Instagram Handle	Website	Product/ Service

Appendix N - Partnership Email Templates

There are many good reasons to enter a business partnership: a partnership can increase revenue, improve brand awareness, broaden your reach, and engage new audiences you didn't have access to before. But before entering a partnership, you have to know what your goals are.

The purpose of a partnership email is to strike up a conversation with your desired partner and, ideally, to make an offer they can't refuse. Simple as that. A good partnership email is personable, convincing and relevant to the receiver. But above all else, it should make it crystal clear what you're offering, what you hope to receive in return and why this partnership is a good idea for the recipient.

Re: Partnership Opportunity I Partnership Company Name + Your Company Name

EXAMPLE ONE:

Coaching Business

Hi X,

Thanks again for your info and letting me connect further with you. :) Please see below and let me know if you have any questions.

[Insert your company pitch here] We are a female-owned local coaching business that works with clients to feel more balanced and reduce day-to-day stress.

We have partnered with multiple yoga spaces before, where we run workshops and support the community to feel more mentally balanced.

I think this would be a strong add-on to [company name] and would support its client base. I am also a huge fan of [company name] and would love to work together!

Would you be interested in discussing a potential partnership or be willing to refer me to someone who would be?

Thank you!

Cheers,
[your name]

EXAMPLE TWO:

Wedding Photography Business

Hi X,

I found you while browsing [website name]. [List something that stands out about them, make it fun and personable]

My name is X, and I [insert unique value proposition - i.e. photograph intimate weddings and elopements in the greater Los Angeles area.] I've attached a PDF to this email with a little more info about me and the clients I enjoy working with, if you'd like to take a peek.

One of the most common questions I get asked from couples is for recommendations for outstanding vendors, and I'd love to have a list of planners and coordinators to recommend... especially for those desert cities! Love going out there.

Currently, I'm growing and expanding my business for the upcoming year and I'm curious if you have any new clients that you're working with?

If you're interested, I'm looking to build some partnerships with vendors I trust. [Provide the business transaction here] For any new clients referred to me by you, I can offer a 5% kickback on whichever package they choose! I work with another wedding photographer here in CA, and we refer each other to work for days we are already booked. So, if Emily sends a rad couple my way, and then they end up booking me, I send Emily a percent of the sale on Venmo! Emily benefits because she was able to provide a recommendation for the couple who she was unable to work with, plus she gets a little cash bonus. And I benefit because I have a rad new client to work with.

[CALL TO ACTION]

Would you have time to chat for about 10-15 minutes this Wednesday at 1:30 or 2:30 pm? Just so we can get to know each other a little better and see how we can help each other out?

Also! If you're ever in the LA area, I'd love to connect in person for coffee or tea sometime :)

Thank you so much for reading and I look forward to your reply!

Cheers,
[your name]

Appendix O - 5-Steps to Your Best Discovery Call

Sales Script

A discovery call is the most crucial part of any sales process. It is a conversation in which you build a relationship with your potential customers and guide them through the transformational journey leading to you making the sale.

The discovery call can occur during various points in the customer's journey. The most important thing to note is that it follows an email, cold call, lead generating campaign, or any other marketing strategy that got the customers curious about your offer. A discovery call is a good way for both you and the prospect to find out if you are a good match for each other. It provides a platform to show you care about the customer's pain points and the solutions you can provide.

Now, a sales script is broken into six scenes to help you feel confident and collected as you sell your coaching packages and close your ideal client!

Scene 1: GREETING

(Super enthusiastic!!)

I.e. I'm thrilled to speak to you today! I'm SO happy that we could connect and that you made the time to reach out, because I know you want to grow.

Scene 2: COMMON GROUND

Rock - reason why person wants to make buying position (understand)

How are things going? (The intention here is to make the client feel comfortable on the call)

- ○ I.e. "....this is a safe space, so please feel fully comfortable because I'm here to help you grow. Whatever you say to me, is only between you and me."

Scene 3: SET THE STAGE

Through this diagnostic, we're going to figure out what areas of your life you need a life coach in. So I'd like to get to know you better. I want to take you through a diagnostic to understand how I can create a custom program to get the best results for you. Part of this investigation is to see if you even need a life coach, and if you don't, I'd tell you! Because if I think of taking you on as a client and we wouldn't see sizable results in the first 90 days, I won't bring you on....

Scene 4: FULL INVESTIGATION

- **Uncover what they want most.**
  "If you could have everything you want in your life/ business/relationship in the next 6 months, what would that look and feel like?"

- **Help them connect emotionally to their vision.**
  "What would _______ (achieving this specific dream/ goal) do for you?" "And what else?" "And what else?" "How important would you say this is to you on a scale of 1–10?"

- **Ask them to list their challenges or obstacles.**
  "What's stopping you from having this _______?" "And what else?" "And what else?" Resist the impulse to coach them!

- **Help them realize the cost of living with the status quo.**
  "What has it cost you not having_______?" "What impact has that had on you?"

- **Show them the bigger why.**
  "If you could overcome _______ (specific obstacle mentioned) what would that do for you?" "And what else?"

- **Gather the gems.**
  "What have you taken away from our conversation so far?"

- **Show them how much it's worth to change.**
  "So, if you were going to put a dollar amount on achieving <u>that</u> goal, what would you say it's worth over the next 2 years? 50K, 100K?"

- **Invite them in.**
  "Are you ready to hear how I can help you achieve _______(their specific dreams and goals)?"
  Share your "system," share your fees & terms, weave in the benefits of working with you and share **success stories** from previous clients.

  Note: during the full investigation use an empathic communication style by doing the following–

1. Mimic – Repeat what the other person said
2. Rephrase – Rephrase their comments to show that you've understood
3. Reflect – Put their feelings into words for them

Scene 5: APPLICATION OF SERVICES

The reason I'm asking you these questions is to better understand the full picture so I can identify how I can help you.

You're in the right place! Are you ready to hear my recommendations and how I can help you create this ideal space?

First let me tell you how I got started...

- Share your personal story (your "WHY") + include analogy:
- Reference your personal why, Simon Sinek for motivation **https://www.youtube.com/watch?v=IPYeCltXpxw**
  - *i.e. We all want to get on the water slide, but sometimes we need that someone to push us to get on. And to get on, is the hardest part! I recognized that people just need a push!! There are so many times that people need a push. The slide is scary – but we need those people in our lives to push us to do scary things because they are the most rewarding parts of our lives. We need those people to force us to do those hard things, or else we're just sitting by the pool!*

Based on what you've said, I recommend my X package... It's a three-month program where we:

1. List out what you will do and month one results
2. List out what you will do and month two results
3. List out what you will do and month three results.

By the end we will (revert back to their initial pain points) and get to (revert back to where they want to be).

Do you have any questions for me? [PAUSE]

What are the next steps?

Scene 6: PATH TO PAYMENT (P2P)

Next steps, we'll send an on-boarding process and schedule our first session. [PAUSE]

HOW MUCH WOULD THAT COST? *(wait for the client to ask this!)*

Speak confidently about your price!

(OBJECTION) Can I talk to my partner?

No problem, why don't we touch base tomorrow after you've talked it over with him. Does the same time tomorrow work for you? In the meantime, I'll email some resources you can look over. (therapy tool, link to website of process, testimonials, etc.).

Next Steps: DO YOU HAVE A FEW MINUTES TO PROCESS PAYMENT OVER THE PHONE?

- a. Do you prefer Zelle or Venmo? (CC has a 3% processing fee)
- b. Send payment request
- c. Collect payment
- d. Email contract and/or invoice

Give them an incentive to pay today! I.e. Day-of 15% discount

Appendix P - The Ten "Did You?" Sales Checklist

Ensure you've completed these 10 steps to quality control for a successful discovery call. If a step is missed it can cost you the new client. Remember, focus on the client - let them uncover their pains and be a strong listener. The checklist will help you close your first client (or second, or third...) with ease and grace and without feeling nervous or sleazy.

- ❑ Did you run through the full investigation and take notes on the language around the prospective clients' pain points, how they want to feel and what it would mean for them to overcome their obstacles?
- ❑ Did you repeat back what they said to help them feel heard? This is called a rephrase.
- ❑ Did you ask them "what else" after they responded?
- ❑ Did you build personal rapport?
- ❑ Did you tell your personal story - and tie it back to the prospect's pain points?
- ❑ Did you share success stories and your unfair advantage after the investigation?
- ❑ Did you stay silent and let them ask you about pricing?
- ❑ Did you ask them their preferred method of payment?
- ❑ Did you offer a day-of discount or add on service to create a sense of urgency to get started?
- ❑ If they concluded with "Let me think about it..." did you ask for an explanation (I.e.is it... connection, price, package content?)?

Appendix Q - Discovery Call Template

Having an email template supports the automation of your business. Make sure to save this as a template in your email so that you can quickly connect with a client as soon as you get an inquiry.

Step 1: First, call the client if a phone number is shared. If you're afraid of calling, know, they probably won't even answer the phone. 95% of people do not answer unknown calls these days.

Step 2: Make the body of the message personable and powerful, describe a little about what you'll do in the consultation call so they know what to expect. Be concrete and specific.

Step 3: Insert your calendly link to avoid the back and forth in finding a time to connect, this way the client has scheduling options and calendly is optimized to share the calendar invite to both you and the client, with follow up emails and texts to ensure a successful start to your meeting

Note: must-haves: link to scheduling tool, client testimonial links, personable touch

Re: Consultation I Client Name + Company Name

Hi Aaron,

Just tried calling you!

I saw your message on [insert platform in which they found you], looking for a coach to help you with massive accountability and bridging the gap between where you are now and where you'd like to be. I also had a look at your certifications and courses on LinkedIn and it's quite impressive!

I'd be happy to get to know you better and see how I can support your kick-ass goals. The easiest path forward would be to schedule a time where we can chat for 15-30 minutes using the link here [insert access to calendar].

Lastly, feel free to take a peek at *just some of the testimonials* [insert link to testimonials page] I have collected from some of my happy clients before our call!

Let me know if you have any questions. Can't wait to connect!

Cheers,
[your name]

Appendix R - Four Post Discovery Call Templates

Send your prospect a follow up email within 24 hours of contact. Especially if they hesitated in signing up, stating I need to.... "think about it," "discuss with a spouse," "shop around".... Coaches often skip the follow-up step so it will help set you apart from the competition. Make sure that your email includes the agreed time to check-in, addresses client goals, includes your social channels and links to testimonials..

Note: Research shows that within one hour, people will have forgotten an average of 50 percent of the information you presented. Within 24 hours, they have forgotten an average of 70 percent of new information, and within a week, forgetting an average of 90 percent of it. Conclusion? Send that follow up email ASAP! ;)

EXAMPLE 1:
CAREER FOCUSED 1

Re: To purpose, growth and confidence I Client Name + Toussi International

Hi Crystal,

I wanted to thank you again for sharing your story and goals around your career growth.

As mentioned, I've included a customized proposal based on your needs. My job as your coach is to be your strategic thought partner to support you in getting just some of the following tangible results:

- Become clear on your career roadmap filled with growth, challenge and development
- Explore jobs that tap into your unique abilities and define your next role
- Create a strategy blueprint to meet financial + personal goals
- Identify what you value in a career to set you up for long-term success
- Ensure your skills/strengths resonate with your next position

Lastly, feel free to look through some success stories from clients [insert link] and on my website.

Look forward to speaking to you Thursday, Crystal!

Best,
[Your name]

EXAMPLE 2: CAREER FOCUSED 2

Re: To purpose, growth and confidence I Client Name + Toussi International

Hi Lígia,

It was lovely speaking with you yesterday! Thank you for opening up about your personal journey and your career and business goals. Making a difference in the world and helping others is your soul's purpose for being here and I don't take such things lightly!

During the next 6 months, I will support you in finding the strategy, structure and focus in **1. Find a career as an assistant psychologist and get set up for success 2. Create the steps to**

organize your life and get you closer to your 5-year goals 3. improve your personal growth and tap into the best version of you.

In our sessions, we will be creating an action plan of how to find a job you love, get your business venture off the ground and tap into your best self. This also includes the **personalized life script** which helps you truly focus on what you want most to set clear intentions and make that a reality. This process creates a visualization that empowers you to align your inspired action to open up greater abundance and success.

Our sessions will be used to cover the following areas (to be fully customized during our discovery session):

1. Jobs that meet your financial, development needs
1a. CV review, LinkedIn update, job search strategies, confidence boosters, interview techniques
2. Create strategy to organize your life in a way that helps you feel satisfied with career and well-being
3. Create positive structure and routine to tap into organization and satisfaction
4. Set SMART targets around goals (this will include lots of homework)
5. Create the steps in starting your own business through a marketing strategy, business model and finding new clients
6. Establish new habits and embrace the best you

The **Career Evolution** program is an all-inclusive transformational program to set you up for success. As mentioned:

- This coaching package is created to maximize growth and implement lasting positive habits and routines
- We meet 3-4x a month for 55 minutes over 6 months
- You have both a *strategy session folder*, accountability assignments and *email and text support* in between sessions.

I also wanted to share a testimonial from a physician that worked with the NHS, and through our sessions, became a resident at UPenn Hospital. His testimonial can be found [insert link]. And of course, more testimonials can also be found [insert link].

Lastly, as mentioned, **please send me your CV to review** before we get started. Also, to clarify about your question, we can either 1. edit your CV together, or 2. I can do it on my own and then get your feedback. We want to be specific with results focused to match the job description provided

Can't wait to get started with you on **Tuesday, 26 May**. If you have ANY questions in the meantime, please feel free to email me or WhatsApp at xxx.xxx.xxxx

Best,
[Your name]

EXAMPLE 3:
BUSINESS FOCUSED

Re: To purpose, growth and confidence I Client Name + Toussi International

Hi Sofia,

It was such a pleasure to connect with you this morning!

I really wanted to thank you for sharing more about your purpose for starting your coaching practice and the direction you'd like to take it.

As mentioned, I've attached the Business Coaching 6-month framework which will be individualized to **your needs** and customized to meet your goals.

My job is to be your thought partner and co-pilot to support you with **practical guidance, definition and strategy** where we'll dive into the following topics:

Personal Growth

- Create an offering to resonate with the intended target
- Identify personal values and ensure this is rolled out to your client

Time Management & Vision

- Master time management techniques to maintain a happy/healthy life
- Prioritize most important tasks aimed to meet monthly & quarterly goals

Business Organization

- Gain clarity on brand positioning and business structure
- Identify and work towards your 1-5 year goal
- Create a strong business plan and unique value proposition
- Implement proven best-practice systems, strategies, templates and tools to grow your business

Marketing

- Formulate a content marketing strategy and plan for execution
- Update/refine website and social channels
- Identify your ideal client and marketing tactics

Pricing

- Feel strong about your pricing structure
- Find a pricing formula to guarantee consistent income

Lastly, I've also attached a *business questionnaire* to help explore your business ideas. When you open it, don't be overwhelmed! (It will be tempting...) I want you to feel relaxed and write free flow, incomplete sentences, bullet points, or whatever works for you. You'll see I ask questions from various angles; this is to help me get a 360 degree view of you and your work. Bear with them and just answer as much as you can. We'll use this as a core document to create a marketing strategy and we'll dive deeper into it during our sessions. Also, if you have time to braindump and send it back to review - I'd love to see your initial focus.

I know you can't make Friday at 10. Is there a time on Thursday, in the late afternoon, that would work to connect?

Feel free to watch some success stories from clients [insert link] and let me know if you have ANY questions in the meantime. Please also confirm receipt so I know you got my email!

Best,
[Your name]
[*Insert business questionnaire attachment*]

EXAMPLE 4: General Area
OUT OF BUDGET

Hi Name,

Thank you for taking the time to discuss working with me as your business coach yesterday. I love getting to know amazing heart-centered entrepreneurs like you.

I just wanted to send a quick follow up and see if you had any final questions about the business coach service?

I remember you are looking for someone who can help you run the back-side of your business, so you can enjoy all that free time you've heard about other online coaches raving about. I know you're at a boiling point where your income can't go up, because you physically (and emotionally) can't do any more of the "work." That's exactly why I became a business coach, to help you go from exhausted and burnt out from focusing on tasks you don't enjoy doing; to focusing on your sweet spot of coaching clients.

I know it's a big decision, so please let me know if you'd like to jump on another call so I can answer any questions tomorrow. Does tomorrow at 12 PM or 4 PM work for you?

I look forward to hearing from you,
[Your name]

Appendix S -
Life Purpose Questionnaire

1. What makes you smile?

2. What have been your favorite things to do in the past?

3. What are your favorite things to do now?

4. What activities make you lose track of time?

5. What inspires you most?

6. What are you naturally good at?

7. What do people typically ask you for help in?

8. If you had to teach something, what would you teach?

9. What would you regret not fully doing, being or having in your life?

10. You are now 90 years old, sitting on a rocking chair outside your porch, you can feel the spring breeze gently brushing against your face. You are blissful and happy, pleased with the wonderful life you've been blessed with. Looking back at your life and all that you've achieved and acquired, all the relationships

you've developed; what matters to you most? List them out.

11. What are your deepest values?

12. What challenge(s) are you facing? How are you overcoming the challenge(s)?

13. What causes do you strongly believe in? Connect with?

14. If you could get a message to a large group of people, who would those people be? What would your message be?

15. Given your talents, passions and values, how could you use these resources to serve, to help, to contribute? (to people, beings, causes, organization, environment, planet, etc.?)

PERSONAL MISSION STATEMENT: *One to two lines of your value statement.*

Appendix T -
Coaching Agreement

This Agreement for Coaching Services ("Agreement") is entered into on this ___ day of ____________________, _____ by and between Sami Toussi ("Coach") and ____________________ ("Client"). In consideration of the mutual covenants, and upon the conditions, set forth herein, the Client requests and the Coach agrees to provide coaching services as follows:

Commitment: Coaching is a structure that facilitates the process of personal and professional development.

Coaching is an ongoing relationship between a Coach and a Client. The Client and Coach agree that the coaching relationship will be designed together. By entering this relationship, the Coach and Client acknowledge that the Client wants to make significant progress and change in his/her life. Because progress and change happen at rates that are unique to each individual, the Coach and Client commit to working with each other for an initial six-month period. This allows the coaching relationship necessary time to develop and progress through objectives, obstacles and successes that occur.

Client acknowledges that the Services are not a guarantee of results. Client is solely responsible for creating and implementing his/her own physical, mental and emotional well-being, decisions, choices, actions, and results. As such, Client agrees that Coach will not be liable for any actions or inaction, or for any direct or indirect result or effect of any Services provided by Coach. Client understands coaching is not therapy, does not substitute for therapy, and does not prevent, cure, or treat any mental disorder or medical disease, and that coaching is not to be used as a substitute for professional advice by legal, mental, medical, financial or other qualified professionals.

Rescheduling Sessions: Rescheduling a coaching session is easily done with appropriate notice. Please allow for at least 24 hours' notice to make appointment changes. If you miss a session without providing a minimum of 24 hours' notice, no refund will be given and the session will be charged at the regular rate.

Confidentiality: The coaching relationship is built on trust. The Coach agrees to keep all conversations and information with the Client private and confidential. No personal ideas, information or thoughts expressed will be shared with anyone except with the permission of the Client.

Referrals: Referrals are the best compliment any coach can receive! If the Client knows someone who could benefit from coaching, the Coach asks that the Client simply refers him or her to the Coah's website where they can contact the Coach directly and will receive a complimentary consultation. The referred should mention the Client's name. For a referral that becomes a client and registers for the Coach's six-month program, a credit of two (2) free 50-minute coaching sessions will be given to the Client.

Payment: All coaching sessions are paid for through digital wallet, Venmo or wire transfer 72 hours before the session. Any invoice not paid on time, by the invoice due date, is subject to a late fee. If an invoice is not paid within 3 business days of the due date, without notice or communication to the Coach, it is subject to a late fee of $25 per day.

Indemnification The Client agrees to indemnify, defend and protect the Coach from and against all lawsuits and costs of every kind pertaining to the Client's business including reasonable legal fees due to any act or failure to act by the Client based upon the Coaching Services.

No Modification Unless in Writing No modification of this Agreement shall be valid unless in writing and agreed upon by both Parties.

Cancellation Fee: The agreed program fee is only refundable if Client gives at least a 72 hours' cancellation notice before the FIRST appointed session. Otherwise, the program fee is non-refundable in all other cases. The program can be postponed based on Coach and Client's availability. IN WITNESS WHEREOF, the parties hereto have executed this Agreement as of the date first above written. **AGREEMENT** I (please print **SECTION** your name)..

I have read, understand and agree to the above terms and conditions:

Coach: _______________________________

Client: _______________________________

Website: _______________________________

Email: _______________________________

Appendix U - New Client Data Form

Date:
Name:
Occupation:
Business Name:
Preferred Address:
E-Mail Address:
Billing Address:
Phone:
Preferred means of communication:

Date of birth:

Important people in client's life (spouse, partner, parents, children, friends, etc.)

Emergency Contact:

How did you hear about my coaching services?

What has brought you to coaching?

Have you ever been coached? If so, please describe your experience.

Where would you rate yourself on a scale from 1 – 10 in the following areas (10-being great, 1-being not great):

Health -

Career/Business -

Finances -

Relationships -

Time Management -

Personal Growth -

Family -

Attitude -

What are you interested in accomplishing in your life in the next 1 to 5 years?

What are one-three things would you like to work on with your coach?

Why is this moment the right time to invest in your career, dreams and goals?

Explain your main roles and responsibilities day-to-day (special relationships, duties, interests).

What parts of life do you enjoy the most?

What seems to need the most improvement in your life?

How do you like to start your day?

Appendix V - Invoice Template

COACHING PROGRAM
CLIENT NAME

Coach:	Your Name
E-mail:	name@company.com
Date:	July 22 2022
PO Number:	PO-00004

INVOICE

SECTION 1: SCOPE OF WORK

- ***Lifetime access to a library of information,*** including tools and resources such as: **(insert details here....)** session takeaways, unique ability strategies, confidence tools, resume reviews, strengths finder techniques and worksheets to support your career growth.
- ***One-on-one private coaching,*** **(insert details here....)** including 10 (ten) strategy and advisory sessions over the course of three to four months.
- ***(OPTIONAL) Unlimited email support*** between coaching sessions to keep you well-supported and on track.

Total Value: $XYZ

New Client Discount: $XYZ

SECTION 2: PAYMENT DETAILS

Payment must be made 48 hours prior to session start date through the following:

Zelle (Account: **XYZ**)

Venmo (Account: **XYZ**)

PayPal (Account: **XYZ**)

Coach: Client:

____________________   ____________________

Appendix W - Credit Card Authorization Form

Today's date: ________/________/__________

I: ____

❏ I hereby authorize this card to be used for all strategy sessions throughout the course of the coaching program.

Credit Card Information

Name as it appears on the Card: _________________________

Type of Card:

☐ VISA ☐ MASTERCARD ☐ DISCOVER ☐ AMERICAN EXPRESS

Credit Card Number: _________________________________

Expiration Date: ______/________

Security Code BACK of Visa OR Master Card (3 digits): ________

Security Code FRONT of Amex Card (4 digits): _____________

Credit Card Billing Address:

Street: ____

City:____________State:____________Zip Code:____________

Telephone: ____

Cardholder or Company Representative:

Signature: _______________________________________

Date: _________/_________/___________

Appendix X - Pre-Session Form

Preparing for the coaching session will allow you to optimize your results and our time together. Prior to the session you may wish to answer the following questions.

1. How was your week?

2. What do you want to get out of our session?

3. What actions did you take after our last session?

4. What were your wins & challenges?

5. What do you want to be held accountable for?

6. What issues do you want to discuss deeper in our session today?

7. Anything else?

Appendix Y -
Check-In Form

CLIENT NAME

1. What results have you achieved since we started our work together?

2. How can I be of further support to your growth?

3. Is there anything you would like to see done differently? If so, what?

4. What has been the most supportive for your growth so far?

Thank you!

Appendix Z - Feedback Form

CLIENT NAME

1. How would you describe your coaching experience thus far?
2. What do you like most about our coaching sessions?
3. What do you like least?
4. How do you feel about the structure of the program?
5. What are your thoughts on how the timeline is progressing?
6. What results have you achieved since we started our work together?
7. What's the outcome you would like to achieve in future sessions?
8. Is there anything you would like to see done differently? If so, what?
9. What has been the most supportive for your growth so far?
10. Anything else you'd like me to know?

Thank you!

Appendix Z.A - Testimonial Request Template

A testimonial is an essential element of content marketing. Testimonials are sales tools, but more than that, they provide social proof. They are used to showcase your company's work and its reputation.

Testimonials work because they aren't strong sales pitches, they come across in an unbiased voice and establish trust. You're using real people to show success in your product or service. You should be using testimonials from past clients to help establish credibility with prospective clients.

See below for an email template to share with your clients to request for a testimonial and feedback from your coaching sessions. Note: it includes an incentive to further expand your clientele and branding.

Example 1:

Re: Testimonial + Feedback Form I Client name + Company Name

Hi Client!

I want to reiterate how much I enjoy working with you on/to *[specify the 2-3 types of focus activities you've been working through/results received here].*

Would you mind posting a testimonial on a few sites? You can simply copy, paste as there are so many different avenues to market yourself these days.

Yelp
Google Business
Facebook
Thumbtack

Please complete by *[share date within 7-10 days from email received]* as I'm trying to get all marketing efforts crossed off by then. Also, as a gift to you (as you're giving to me!), I would be happy to give a 45-minute session to someone you care about who you think could use support during this time.

I'd also LOVE some input from our strategy sessions thus far, and would appreciate it if you would fill in the Qs in the feedback form attached. This can also be supportive in writing the review!

Cheers,
Your Name
Instagram: @
Website:
LinkedIn:

Example 2:

Re: Testimonial I Daniel + Toussi International

Hi Daniel,

Hope you're having a great start to your week!

I wanted to get some feedback from our career coaching program and would appreciate it if you can take the time to answer the questions listed in the google form link here.

Secondly, I'd be so grateful if you would post a testimonial of our work together on some of the marketing channels below. You can simply copy, paste as there are so many different avenues to market yourself these days.

Yelp
Google Business
Facebook
Thumbtack

LinkedIn - request shared over platform

Thank you so much again, Daniel! Speak to you next week!

Best,
Sami
Instagram: @
Website:
LinkedIn:

Appendix Z.B - Closing Questions I Final Coaching Session

Below are some questions to verbally ask your clients during the last session of their coaching program. Alternatively, you can send this within a final coaching feedback form. Remember, this gives both you an opportunity to take note of their successes from your coaching (metrics to share with new clients, promote on website, feel professional validation) as well as topics to focus on as you pitch next steps of coaching together.

1. What have you achieved/are proud of during the coaching period? (think broadly)
2. What specifically have you achieved or are doing differently as a direct result of the coaching? (review goals here)
3. What are your top 3 goals and dreams in life right now? (personal AND work)
4. What are your top 5 priorities in life as you now understand them?
5. What limiting beliefs have you let go of (eg. about yourself, life, others)? I NO LONGER BELIEVE:
6. What positive new beliefs do you have (eg. about yourself, life, others)? I NOW BELIEVE:
7. What specifically have you learned about yourself? (that you perhaps haven't mentioned yet)
8. How is your life different as a result of the learnings you have made during the coaching period?
9. What have you learned that you will carry forward in life?
10. What has been the best bit of coaching you received?
11. What are the best things about your life?

12. If you were to give yourself a message or mantra to carry forward and sum everything up, what would it be?
13. What else would you like to note down that would be useful for me going forward?

Bonus I Workflow Scripts

Calendly is your one-stop shop to easily schedule discovery calls. Their Personalized Workflow function helps you automate the client experience. See below scripts to ensure a personalized and supportive quality service before your prospect becomes a new client!

In an event when you need to cancel a consultation appointment.

EMAIL I CONSULTATION CANCELLATION/ RESCHEDULE

Email notifications will be sent to your invitee if you cancel the event.

Canceled: {{event_name}} with {{my_name}} on {{event_date}}

Hi {{invitee_full_name}},

Hope you're doing well! Apologies but the Toussi International calendar wasn't updated accordingly and your {{event_name}} at {{event_time}} on {{event_date}} has been rescheduled.

Please confirm the new time works well for you!

In the meantime, feel free to look through some client success stories here.

Best,

Toussi International Team

Instagram
LinkedIn
Profile Details

TEXT REMINDER I BEFORE CONSULTATION

Reminder: {{event_name}} with {{my_name}} at {{event_time}} on {{event_date}}

See you soon! -Toussi International Team

EMAIL REMINDER I BEFORE CONSULTATION

An invitee will receive a reminder email before a scheduled event at specified times.

Subject: Reminder: Strategy Consultation with Sami Toussi at 3 PM on July 27 2022

Hi Invitee First Name,

This is a friendly reminder that your Event Name with My Name is at Event Time on Event Date.

Location

Event Description

Questions And Answers

In case you have trouble logging in, please send Sami a message at info@samitoussi.com

Best,

Toussi International Team

Instagram
LinkedIn
Profile Details

[Timing: 24 hours before, 8 hours before]

POST CONSULT I EMAIL FOLLOW UP

Subject: To further growth! I Toussi International Consultation

Hi Invitee First Name,

It was great connecting with you today!

I wanted to thank you again for opening up about your goals and sharing your journey with me.

I really connected with you and know our work together can bridge the gap between where you are now and where you want to go.

Please let me know if you have any feedback or additional requests from the coaching offering.

Lastly, feel free to look through client success stories here!

Best,

Sami Toussi

Instagram
LinkedIn
Profile Details